And the house of Israel called the name thereof Manna: and it was like coriander seed, white; and the taste of it was like wafers made with honey.

—Exodus 16:31 (KJV)

MYSTERIES & WONDERS of the BIBLE

Unveiled: Tamar's Story
A Life Renewed: Shoshan's Story
Garden of Secrets: Adah's Story
Among the Giants: Achsah's Story
Seeking Leviathan: Milkah's Story
A Flame of Hope: Abital's Story
Covenant of the Heart: Odelia's Story
Treacherous Waters: Zahla's Story
Star of Wonder: Dobah's Story
Sweet Gift from Heaven: Rana's Story

MYSTERIES & WONDERS of the BIBLE

SWEET GIFT FROM HEAVEN
RANA'S STORY

Anne Davidson

A Gift from Guideposts

Thank you for your purchase! We want to express our gratitude for your support with a special gift just for you.

Dive into **Spirit Lifters**, a complimentary e-book that will fortify your faith, offering solace during challenging moments. Its 31 carefully selected scripture verses will soothe and uplift your soul.

Please use the QR code or go to **guideposts.org/ spiritlifters** to download.

Mysteries & Wonders of the Bible is a trademark of Guideposts.

Published by Guideposts
100 Reserve Road, Suite E200
Danbury, CT 06810
Guideposts.org

Copyright © 2025 by Guideposts. All rights reserved. This book, or parts thereof, may not be reproduced, stored in a retrieval system, or transmitted in any form or by any means, electronic, mechanical, photocopying, recording, or otherwise, without the written permission of the publisher.

This is a work of fiction. While the characters and settings are drawn from scripture references and historical accounts, apart from the actual people, events, and locales that figure into the fiction narrative, all other names, characters, places, and events are the creation of the author's imagination or are used fictitiously. Every attempt has been made to credit the sources of copyrighted material used in this book. If any such acknowledgment has been inadvertently omitted or miscredited, receipt of such information would be appreciated.

Scripture references are from the following sources: *The Holy Bible, King James Version* (KJV). *The Holy Bible, New International Version* (NIV). Copyright © 1973, 1978, 1984, 2011 by Biblica, Inc. Used by permission of Zondervan. All rights reserved worldwide. www.zondervan.com.

Cover and interior design by Müllerhaus
Cover illustration by Brian Call represented by Illustration Online LLC.
Typeset by Aptara, Inc.

ISBN 978-1-961442-09-2 (hardcover)
ISBN 978-1-961442-10-8 (softcover)
ISBN 978-1-961442-11-5 (epub)

Printed and bound in the United States of America
10 9 8 7 6 5 4 3 2 1

MYSTERIES & WONDERS of the BIBLE

SWEET GIFT FROM HEAVEN
RANA'S STORY

CAST OF CHARACTERS

Asim • a member of the Medjay, Pharaoh's police force

Batya • a troublemaker in the Hebrew camp

Chava • a Hebrew woman who owns a beautiful bracelet

Gideon • one of Joshua's soldiers

Keziah • a young woman in the Hebrew camp, Rana's friend

Leah • a spinner, and a woman of faith

Moses • leader of the Hebrew people

Rana • an Egyptian street thief and pickpocket

Shimon • a stonecutter

Zoser • the Egyptian who buys stolen goods from thieves

GLOSSARY OF TERMS

abba • Hebrew word for father

Ammit • in the underworld, the Devourer of the Dead, consumes the hearts of sinners

Atum • the Egyptian god of the evening, all things arose from him. Pithom is dedicated to him.

Duat • the Egyptian underworld or afterlife

Elim • an oasis

Geb • Egyptian earth god

Goshen • the district where the Hebrew slaves lived

Hathor • one of the most powerful Egyptian gods, the goddess of beauty

horned viper • a venomous species of snake

Horus • Egyptian god of the sky

imma • a Hebrew word for mom

Isis • wife of Osiris, Egyptian goddess of the afterlife

kem • the silt left by the Nile's annual flooding

khamsin • a sandstorm

Kohn • the Egyptian moon god

manna • a miraculous, edible substance provided to the Hebrews during their time in the desert by God. It was white, and the size of a coriander seed. The name derives from the words "man hu," which means "What is it?"

Marah • the place of bitter water

Medjay • Pharaoh's police force

Nekhbet • goddess with the head of a vulture and the body of a woman, protector of pharaohs, queens, and children

Nephthys • an Egyptian goddess, guardian of the household

Nu • an Egyptian god who represents primordial chaos

Nut • Egyptian sky god

Osiris • one of the most important Egyptian gods. God of the underworld, death, resurrection

Pithom • Pharaoh's treasure city, near Goshen where many of the Hebrews live

Ra • Egyptian god of the sun

Raamses • another of Pharaoh's treasure cities

Season of Inundation • also called Ahket, the time of the year when the Nile floods, from mid-September to early January

Sekhmet • the lion-headed Egyptian goddess of healing

Set • Egyptian god of deserts and disorder, a thief

Shai • the Egyptian god of good fortune

Shu • Egyptian god of the air

Tefnut • a goddess, Shu's sister

tiger nut sweets • an Egyptian confection made with dates, nuts, honey, and cinnamon

Tum • Egyptian god of the setting sun

Wilderness of Shur • where the Hebrews emerged from the Red Sea

CHAPTER ONE

It would take more than the waters of the mighty Nile turning into blood to frighten Rana. It would take more than locusts, or hail and fire raining down from the sky, or even three days of total darkness. Fear? That did not come from the plagues the Hebrew slaves believed were sent by their God. Fear came from hunger and from want. Fear rose in her on those nights when she slept on the ground, her feet cold, the stars glittering like knives above, and she found herself wondering if—at some time she could no longer remember—she ever had a home and a family.

Even that morning when the people at the marketplace cried and wailed and talked about what had happened the night before, when the God of the Hebrews prowled the land of Egypt like a hungry lion and killed its firstborn, she was not afraid. She was alive. She was a survivor. Her strength and her cleverness, that was what kept the fear at bay.

When she was yet a child, she learned to be quick and quiet so that she might pilfer bread from the sellers at the market or snatch up a trinket or two from the homes of the wealthy. Since she had come into her womanhood, she had discovered how her smile could dazzle men in the taverns so that they forgot the grilled wild fowl they ate, and the beer they drank, and the fact that their purses were within easy reach of her nimble fingers.

A survivor, yes, as she would be that day and always.

Telling herself not to forget it, she waited while a small, bent man at the market stall in Pharaoh's treasure city of Pithom fell into conversation with an old woman whose cheeks were stained with tears.

"My son, my son!" The old woman's hands were like claws, and she twisted them together and wept. "Taken from me in the dark. And his oldest gone too. I am a widow, and my son and my grandson cared for me. What will I do now?"

"You will do all you have to," Rana whispered, not because the woman could hear her but to remind herself. "Just as I do." The man put his hand on the woman's shoulder to console her, and they cried together, and Rana saw her opportunity. There was a basket nearby piled with amulets made in the shape of lizards. Pretty, shiny things. The treasure city of Pithom was dedicated to Atum, god of the evening sun, and the lizard was sacred to him. If she could scoop up five or more of the baubles and sell them to Zoser, the one-eyed man always eager to accept what she brought him and ask no questions, she could eat bread and drink beer for three days. She would not need to live with the hunger.

Her gaze fixed on the man and the old woman, she snaked a hand to the basket. It was early, the metal charms were cool to the touch, and she snatched up a handful of them. She was just about to tuck them under her linen sheath when she heard voices raised behind her.

"Stop! Thief!"

Rana's heart slammed against her ribs, yet she stood as still as the statue of the Pharaoh—all life and praise to him!—that looked over the nearby complex of buildings where grain was stored. She dared not look guilty, or she would surely attract attention. But she could not seem unconcerned, either, for that in itself would make her look suspicious. Like the other people in the marketplace, she glanced around to see what the commotion was about.

Now her heart beat in double time, so forcefully she thought it would burst from her chest. Three of the Medjay, Pharaoh's dreaded police, marched toward her, the muscles of their arms and legs bulging in the morning sunlight, their wooden staffs raised, their gazes fixed on Rana.

And in that moment when her breath caught and her blood ran cold, she knew that though the God of the Hebrews did not frighten her, the thought of being captured for her crime did. She did not wish to have her fingers cut off or her nose sliced from her face as punishment.

Rana took off running. Still, she was no fool. She kept a tight grip on the lizard amulets while she darted around the market stall, rushed past a man selling figs, sprinted toward the grain storehouse built with bricks that had been made by the Hebrew slaves from mud and straw. There, she stopped in the shadows, but only long enough to catch her breath. The Medjay were not far away. She could hear them calling to one another, and she was glad they did not have one of their dogs or monkeys with them. Being stopped by the lash of a Medjay rod would be bad enough. Being ripped apart by the teeth of one of their hounds or the claws of a vicious monkey would be even worse.

A second of rest, no more, and she started running again. She did not look over her shoulder. She didn't have to. She heard the footfalls of the Medjay behind her, and, breathless, she whispered a prayer to the great god, Set, who had once stolen the body of Osiris from the embalmer. Being a thief, too, Set would surely understand. Set would rescue her.

When she rounded a corner, she saw the answer to her prayer. A donkey cart blocked her path. Rana was young and limber, so she ducked under the cart, scrambled across the dusty ground, and leaped to her feet on the other side. The Medjay were large men and, even as she heard them yell for the driver to move along, she smiled and thanked Set for his kindness.

She knew she did not have the luxury of basking in her small victory. Here on the far side of the storage buildings were the homes of the craftsmen of Pithom. The painters who decorated Pharaoh's temples. The stonemasons who carved his statues. The dwellings here were small and simple, and from some of them, she heard the wailing of mourners. But one, very close by, was silent, and if it was empty, it would be the perfect place to hide.

No sooner was she through the doorway, though, than Rana froze. This worker was a firstborn son, surely. He lay on his low-slung bed, his cheeks sunken, his vacant eyes staring at the ceiling and the flies that buzzed around his face.

"I am sorry to disturb you," she told him at the same time she knew she could not afford to ignore the opportunity his silence presented. A quick look over her shoulder, and she slipped under the bed.

With her stomach pressed to the earthen floor, she had a unique perspective of the home's doorway. She saw the Medjay rumble past and breathed a sigh of relief. Until she heard one man call to the others to come back.

Three pairs of feet stopped in the doorway. Three rods held at the sides of six muscular legs.

"You think she has come in here?" one of the men asked. "There is death in this house. She would not dare."

"A thief will dare anything if she is desperate enough." The voice of this man was thick and raspy. He stepped into the dwelling and paused, and though Rana could see no more than his reed sandals and muscled shins, she knew he was taking a close look around. "A firstborn son," he said. He was surely looking right at the body, right at the bed.

"They say the Hebrew God is powerful," another of the men replied. "Even Pharaoh trembles before him. He has ordered the Hebrews to leave this land."

"Has he?" The man with the raspy voice spat on the ground. "I had not heard. It seems Pharoah has surrendered too easily."

"With plague upon the land—"

The man with the raspy voice barked a curse. "Pharaoh is a god, is he not? He can exact his own revenge."

"Yes," one of the other men replied. "But now that Pharaoh's own son is dead—"

"Firstborn."

Raspy Voice snapped, "I would see to it that the Hebrews were slaughtered for their insolence."

"They have strong magic," the first man reminded him.

"But our little thief does not. And I tell you this, friends, if I ever see her again, my rod will be the least of her worries." Rana did not need to see his face. She knew it was twisted with anger. Wherever she was, he wanted her to hear. He thundered his words. "I will kill you with my own bare hands, little thief. I will feed your body to the crocodiles in the mighty Nile."

"Then we had best be off and find her." The other two men moved again to the doorway. "Come along, Asim. The sooner we find this thief, the sooner you can use your rod to teach her a lesson."

Asim whipped his wooden rod through the air, and it whooshed and buzzed as Rana squeezed her eyes shut and cringed.

When he and the other Medjay walked out of the dwelling, she released the breath she'd been holding.

She didn't move, not for a very long time, and when she finally pulled herself out from under the bed and went again to the door, she peeked out the doorway, left and right.

There was no sign of the Medjay. "Thank you, great Set," she whispered, as she slipped from the house.

Outside, a woman balancing a basket on her head eyed Rana carefully. A man leading a calf on a tether looked her over. A child, his eyes shining with excitement, pointed a finger. "This is the one," he called out. "The one the Medjay are searching for."

She did not wait to hear more. Had the Medjay gone farther into the district of the craftsmen? Rana ran back toward the marketplace, the way she'd come.

She did not have a plan, at least not at first. It was not until she realized her hand was still gripping the lizard amulets that she knew she might yet find a way to save herself.

With the thief and Medjay gone, the marketplace had settled again into its routine. Women picked at the figs and dates. Men gathered in tight circles, some of them weeping. Others were off to the side, grinding grain. Rana kept herself to the perimeter of the market, her gaze focused ahead of her on the grand temple of Atum. It was a glorious building, and looking at the statues outside it—the pharaohs and gods, huge and majestic—never failed to fill her with awe. But it was not wonderment she was after. Instead, she searched the shadows at the far side of the temple. There, outside one of the outbuildings used by the men who maintained the temple and its environs, she found what she was looking for.

Zoser was a man of substance, the thief all others looked up to, the one who told them where to find the pilgrims with their heavy purses, or the soldiers, drunk on beer and too careless with their gold. He was the one who accepted the items they brought to him. In exchange, he gave them bread, and if the items they presented were especially valuable, he might even offer a place for them to sleep in the courtyard of his home.

Zoser was propped against the building, dozing, his chin on the bulge of his stomach, and Rana wasted no time. She closed in on him and stuck out her hand, revealing the lizard amulets. "I have these."

Her voice started him. His head came up. His right eye had been taken by the Medjay in the days when Zoser himself prowled the streets as Rana did now, and he had to swivel his head and squint with his good eye to see what she held out to him. He sniffed. His fingers were fat, and he wrapped them around Rana's wrist and yanked her hand closer to his good eye. "Worthless," he mumbled.

Rana refused to lose heart. She swallowed hard. "One or two, perhaps, would not be worth your interest. But if I give you all five…"

His eye sparked with sudden interest. "Give?"

She nodded. "All five."

"For what in return?"

"No bread. No beer. Just…" His fingers tightened around her wrist, but Rana did not dare pull her hand away. Zoser had always reminded her of a jackal god, keen and ruthless, yet she refused to let him know the touch of his hand made her insides writhe like a snake. "I want only to take shelter in your dwelling."

When he laughed, Zoser's stomach quivered. "The Medjay are looking for you?"

She nodded.

"What have you done?"

"Just"—she moved her hand as much as she was able—"these."

"Small things. And hardly enough."

"But..." She hated that her voice quavered.

"But..." Zoser put up a hand. "Ten days of thieving. That is my price. You give me these small things, and you spend ten days giving me all you gather. And you ask nothing in return."

It was an outrageous bargain, but Rana knew she had no choice. She tamped down her anger and swallowed the epithets on her tongue. "Yes," she whispered, and when Zoser tilted his head as if he hadn't heard, she raised her voice and spoke again. "Yes, I will do it. But in return, you must—"

"Yes, yes. I know." His hand still tight around her wrist, Zoser hauled himself to his feet with a grunt. He was not a tall man, and when he stood before her, his stout belly nearly touched hers. He gave her a close look, slipped his tongue over his lips, and called out, "I have her! Come collect the thief!"

The three Medjay emerged from the nearby workroom.

Rana's mouth fell open. The breath caught in her throat. "You cannot!" She struggled to free herself from Zoser, but his grip was tight. He grinned. The Medjay, their rods raised, closed in. And

Rana knew she had only one hope. She bit the hand that held her, as hard as she could.

Zoser howled like a hyena, and when he jumped back, he loosened his hold on her, and Rana did not waste a moment. Before the Medjay could get nearer, she whirled and ran.

Past the workers' houses. Through an alleyway. She shot out from between two buildings and found herself in a district she was not familiar with where the dwellings were smaller even than the craftsmen's homes. It was a silent, forlorn place that looked abandoned. No sounds of voices or of the weeping she'd heard earlier. No animals. No people. She leaped over an empty basket in the middle of the pathway. She skirted a pile of broken crockery. She ran until she came to an enclosure, and when she jumped the barrier, she startled a shepherd working at the far end of it to gather his sheep and goats. The man was clothed in wool.

She knew then that she was in the heart of Goshen, where the Hebrew slaves lived, for the Israelite people spun and wove the wool of their animals, while Egyptians made their cloth from linen.

Try as she might, Rana could not remember if she'd ever heard enough about the Hebrews to know if they welcomed or feared the Medjay. If she was discovered, would the slaves hand her over with as much glee as Zoser had?

She couldn't take the chance of finding out.

She darted through the animals and past the shepherd, and because of the quiet, she heard a grunt and curses when one of the Medjay tripped and fell somewhere behind her. The others did not stop, their footfalls echoing through the silence.

Another alleyway, and though she was tempted to stop there, to press herself against the wall and hope she was not discovered, Rana did not. The pathway between the buildings twisted right and left, and she followed it, emerging into a large square engulfed in complete chaos. It was no wonder she had not encountered another soul except the shepherd. It seemed as if all of Goshen was gathered here.

Women and children stacked baskets and textiles into carts to which men hitched mules. Old women hurried by, urns of water on their heads. Children dragged each other by the hand, encouraged by the shouts of their mothers. And all around her, voices were raised in what sounded to Rana like a song of praise, a song of new beginnings and freedom.

Not for her. Not if she was discovered.

Rana looked over her shoulder just in time to see the two remaining Medjay emerge from the alley. She had little time. And few options.

There was a cart up ahead loaded with wool waiting to be spun, and as the man who should be attending it was busy helping an old woman onto the seat at the front of the cart, Rana slipped into the back. She scooted as far from the back of the cart as she was able until she was pressed to the far end of it, grabbing handfuls of wool as she did and piling them in front of her, a wall to shelter and hide her.

"Where is she?" Asim, the Medjay, called out, but no one answered him. They were too busy securing their possessions to the backs of mules, gathering their families, praising their God. "Has anyone seen the thief?" he shouted. "For if you have, you will be rewarded with Pharaoh's gratitude."

In all the turbulence, Rana was surprised to catch a glimmer of laughter from the driver of the cart. "We are free men, setting off on the road and meeting up with Moses and the others who are coming from Raamses. Your pharaoh is our master no longer."

With that, the cart lurched forward. Wherever it was going, Rana knew it didn't matter. She would slip from the cart in the darkness and make her way back to Pithom. For now, though, she was safe.

She, too, was on the road to freedom.

CHAPTER TWO

"If you give me fleas, I will leave you in the desert, and you will have nothing to eat but rocks and sand."

The donkey at Rana's side did not look particularly disturbed by her threat. He flicked an ear. She scratched her arm.

She had never tended a beast. In Pithom, she'd never needed one. Still, she was not about to take chances, not when it came to vermin. When she'd snatched the animal in the enclosure where his owner had bedded him down, she'd tied a rope around his neck. Now, she held onto the rope tighter, even as she moved a step back from the donkey.

She was smart enough to know the animal would need food and water, just as she would, on their journey back to Pithom, and when she gathered bread and fruit—a little from this tent, a little from that—she took enough to share. She'd found some waterskins left unattended outside a tent where a man was snoring and a woman grumbled that he was impossible and she would never get any sleep, but they were full and flung over the creature's back. Now if only he would keep quiet long enough for her to lead him away from the Hebrew camp and into the darkness that filled the wilderness with shadows.

As if he knew exactly what she was thinking and dared to defy her, the donkey tossed his head and snorted. Rana feared he would bray and alert the camp, so she dug into the bag she had tied at her side and offered him a handful of the grain she'd pilfered at the same time she took the beast itself. While he munched, she glanced again over her shoulder, looking toward the camp some few hundred yards behind her. Just as she hoped, the Hebrews were still celebrating, sharing bread and drink, bathed in the radiance of the pillar of fire that guided them through the wilderness each night and, in the daytime, changed into a pillar of cloud to lead them.

The pillar was just one of the wonders she'd seen in the time since they departed Pithom, another she could not explain, and Rana did not even try. She knew only what she'd seen when they came to the Red Sea. She had feared they would be trapped and slain by the Egyptian soldiers who pursued them. Moses, the Hebrew leader, stood on the shore and stretched his arms over the water. Then...

Thinking back on it, Rana gasped.

The waters had parted.

The Hebrews crossed the sea as if on dry land.

"I do not know how their priests make such magic happen," she said, telling the donkey what she'd been thinking in the hours since the Hebrews crossed the sea. The donkey was too busy chewing to care. She let him finish, taking one more look back to where the Hebrews were dancing and singing praise to their God, who had delivered them first from Egypt and then, from certain doom. Their words drifted to her on a chilly breeze.

"The Lord is my strength and my song, and He is become my salvation."

It was the perfect opportunity. At least as far as Rana was concerned. While some danced, others ate. While some tended to the animals that had made the journey with them, a few—like the snoring man who'd left his waterskins outside his tent—rested. What mattered was that the Hebrews were occupied, and so she had time to slip away and make a start on her journey back—

"Home?" The word tasted unfamiliar in Rana's mouth. It must have sounded just as odd to the donkey as it did to her, because he cocked his head and gave her a look, his large brown eyes catching what there was of the light and glimmering at her. "Egypt is where I live," she explained to him. "Where I have always lived. It is where we are going, little donkey, because I do not belong with these people. I am not like them, and if they discover who I really am, I fear I will be left behind in the wilderness. I must return to Egypt. And yet..." Her sigh rippled the early morning air. Her gaze drifted back to the camp and the people who so recently were no more than slaves and now seemed like nothing if not a huge, happy family. "Pithom," she said, more to herself than to the donkey, "never felt like the home I imagine in my dreams."

It was just as well that a cart rumbled somewhere nearby, the noise startling Rana. It gave her a chance to shake the uncomfortable thoughts from her head. She slipped around to the other side of the donkey so she would not be seen, and fleas or no fleas, pressed herself to him to keep him still and keep herself hidden. It was only when she heard the cart stop that she dared to peek around the beast to see what was happening. Beyond an outcropping of boulders, she saw three men leap from the cart. At this distance, she could not make out their faces, but she could see that they were dressed as all the Hebrews were, in woolen tunics. They were much like the one Rana had recently stolen and slipped over her own linen tunic, the better to disguise herself since they'd left Pithom, as she hid first in one cart, then in another, or tried her best to blend in with the many Hebrews who walked alongside their families.

One of the men was tall and burly. Another was reed thin. The third was short and walked with a limp. They retrieved something bulky from the back of the cart and, grunting, the two shorter men balanced it between them and tramped off in the direction the large man pointed. In another minute, all three men were lost to the shadows.

"A cart would be a better way to journey to Egypt, even than a donkey." Rana couldn't help savoring the thought, even if it was impractical. It took her but a moment to come to her senses. If she jumped into the cart and drove it away, she would be seen, she would be heard. Besides, the cart was pulled by a donkey, and as she had already learned from the short time she had been in possession of her own donkey, they were not the swiftest of creatures. She would be apprehended, surely, and she couldn't risk that.

None of that, of course, meant she couldn't get a closer look.

Rana held a finger to her lips, instructing the donkey to keep quiet. She slipped his tether around a nearby rock to keep him from wandering, then ever so slowly crept forward through the darkness, her head cocked, carefully listening for any sounds of the men's return.

Nothing.

She dared a few more steps closer.

Silence.

She slipped behind a boulder. Sidestepped to another. One last deep breath for courage and she darted into the open and closed in. She was hoping for a blanket. Or trinkets she might sell when she got back to Pithom, but the cart was empty except for a small, lumpy sack tucked in one corner. She grabbed it and untied the strings that held it closed, and she didn't have to look inside to know what it contained. She breathed in deep and smelled the wonderful aromas of nuts and dates, honey and spices.

"Tiger nuts sweets!" Her mouth watered. She was just about to pop one of the delicacies into her mouth when she heard the sound of the men's voices. Ever closer. Returning to the cart.

The sack clutched close, she hurried back the way she came, and by the time she returned to where the donkey waited for her, she was out of breath. "I have a treat for us," she told him, and while she hid again behind his bulky body, she thanked the gods who had sent such a glorious surprise and popped a ball of the fragrant confection into her mouth.

The clatter of the cart drew closer and the sweet stuck in Rana's throat. She didn't know if the laws of the Hebrews were as rigid as those of her Egyptian countrymen. If she was discovered with the stolen donkey and the bag of sweets, would she be whipped? Put to death? She did not intend to find out.

"Quiet, donkey." She pressed him closer and found a strange comfort in his warmth.

Provided there were no fleas.

"We will wait until they are long gone," she whispered, and as if he understood, he stomped a hoof. "And once they are, we will share a tiger nut sweet and then be on our way."

She was as good as her word. After all, a promise is a promise, even when it is made to a donkey. Once the cart rumbled back toward the camp, she took another sweet from the bag, bit it in half, and fed the other half to the donkey. With both of them cheered by the taste of the treat, she took the rope and led him west, further into the darkness, ever closer to Egypt.

She could not say how long she walked. Rana only knew that soon she found herself at the shore of the Red Sea. It had looked so different from her vantage point in the cart where she had hidden herself during the crossing, so easy to traverse when Moses held out his arms and the waters parted. Now, she stood in awe of the water spread out before her.

"It is even mightier than the Nile," she told the donkey, but then, she imagined he could see that for himself. There were places along the sacred Nile where a person standing on one shore could easily see a person on the other side. Not here. She saw that it was a vast, unending sea. She saw something else too, and her heart clutched and her stomach swooped.

Though she knew from the excited talk of the Hebrews that they had somehow managed to evade the army that pursued them, she was in the forefront of the escaping Hebrews and had not seen what happened behind them. She did not know how their freedom had been secured. Until now.

Now she saw smashed pieces of chariots floating in the water. And a sword that bobbed for a moment on the surface then was swallowed by the waves. Around her where the water lapped the shore, bits and pieces of charioteers' brass armor dotted the ground like fallen stars. There was only one explanation.

"We came on dry land," she told the donkey, who had certainly made the trip and knew as much. "But now there is no dry land. The water that parted for the Hebrews closed behind them and swallowed their enemies. It is no wonder they sing the praises of their God. He has protected them. Delivered them."

As quickly as she was filled with wonder, though, the emotion drained. Rana's shoulders drooped. A knot blocked her throat.

Their God may have delivered the Hebrews, but when He closed the water around their pursuers, He left Rana with a donkey, water, food, tiger nut sweets—and no way back to Egypt.

Her knees gave way, and Rana slumped to the ground, and blackness and despair closed around her like a hand, choking her. She sat for a long time, her head propped against the donkey's leg, her mind filled with black thoughts, and when she came again to her senses, her cheeks were wet with tears.

"We have no way back to Egypt," she told the donkey. "Not when the way we came is flooded again. We have no choice. We must return to the Hebrew camp."

Disappointment was nothing new. Not in Rana's life. Like each time it had happened before, she knew there would be no rescue, not unless she found a way to rescue herself, so she shook her shoulders, scraped her knuckles over her eyes, and stood.

"Come, donkey." She tugged his rope. "It is time for you to go back to your pen. And me?" As if he'd actually asked the question, she gave the donkey a look. "I will think of another way to get back to where I belong. For now…" She led him eastward. "If the Hebrews are still celebrating, I think they will not notice one more person around their fires. At least there, I will find food and drink. I think even a donkey can understand what a blessing that is."

She told herself not to forget it, and they scrambled again over the dusty ground, back to where they started. By the time they got there, the sun was over the horizon, coloring the rocky ground with crimson, touching the tops of the nearby mountains with a gold that did not shine nearly as bright as the pillar of fire over the camp. A wind whipped the air and dust erupted around her, and Rana closed her eyes and turned away. When she looked back again, the pillar of fire had turned to cloud.

With the coming of daylight, the camp was alive with cooks and shepherds, bakers and spinners, and she considered her options. There was a group nearby still celebrating, young people mostly, those with enough energy to cross the Red Sea and still dance the next morning. She would return the donkey to his pen and do her best to blend in with the dancers.

The better to assure her anonymity, she pulled her headscarf—the one she'd taken at the same time she'd pilfered her woolen tunic—closer. She couldn't afford to arouse suspicion. She'd seen what the Hebrew God did to the enemies of His people. How might those people treat an Egyptian donkey thief? Eager to rid herself of the animal, she'd just made a move toward the donkey's pen when she heard a man's voice close behind her.

"You there! Woman! Where are you going with that donkey?"

Rana's breath caught. Her insides went cold. It was impossible to pretend she hadn't heard the man, so before she turned to him, she pasted on a smile.

It wavered around the edges when she found herself facing a tall Hebrew with muscular arms and a dark beard trimmed close to his square, stubborn chin. He had a sword tied around his waist, a bow hung over his left shoulder, and a scowl on his face the likes of which she hadn't seen since she'd gone up against the Medjay back in Pithom.

Her heart skipped a beat.

"The donkey..." As if he might provide the answer for her, she looked toward the beast. "I am putting him away in his pen, of course."

"Then why is he packed as if for a journey?" the man wanted to know.

"Why do you ask?"

He narrowed his eyes. "It is my business to ask such questions."

"But not mine to answer them. Not when they are so silly that you would surely know the answer without asking if only you had stopped to think about it. I needed to refill our waterskins, and it is easier to take a donkey than it is to carry the skins. I think you will agree."

"Of course, but—"

"And now that the skins are full, I will reward the donkey for his hard work." To prove it, she put a hand in the sack at her side and scooped up a handful of grain and offered it to the donkey, who gladly accepted it. "Then I will spread out what straw we have so that he can sleep. I, too, may need some rest." As if it was true, she stretched and yawned. "We had a long trek through the waters last night, didn't we? And today, I am weary. Do you know how long we will camp here?"

"No one has said."

"Then we might be moving on soon. All the more reason to get some rest today." She grabbed the donkey's rope to turn him toward his home. "You would hardly begrudge us that."

For a heartbeat, two, she was sure she had been skilled enough in her lies to convince him. It wasn't until she saw his lips pull tight that she knew he wasn't done with her.

"What family do you come from?" he wanted to know.

"They are waiting for me." She looked toward the revelers around the closest fire. Not a lie. Not this time. She didn't say she was one of them.

"Your name?"

She had never been good at playing at the sort of trifling games she'd seen other women use on men. But that didn't mean she hadn't been paying attention. That she hadn't been watching and learning. She raised an eyebrow, lifted her lips in what she hoped looked like a flirtatious smile. "I might ask you the same."

He narrowed his eyes and squared his shoulders. "I am Gideon. One of Joshua's soldiers."

"And a busy man, no doubt, who surely has better things to do than make conversation with a woman and her donkey."

She didn't wait for him to stop her again. The rope twisted around her hand and, concealing the way it shook, she steered the donkey back where he belonged. She didn't linger, just shooed him into the pen where she'd found him hours earlier, ignoring the silly pang inside her that made her feel like she was abandoning a friend.

When the donkey brayed, she did not turn around to say a final goodbye. Rana had slipped away once before, without anyone noticing the donkey was gone. Now she slipped away again before anyone could take note of the fact that he was back, quickly and quietly and long before anyone ever noticed she'd been there.

CHAPTER THREE

"We depart tomorrow to cross the Wilderness of Shur."

"The Wilderness of Shur. At first light tomorrow."

"Be ready. Be packed. We leave just as the pillar of fire turns to cloud in the morning."

All around the camp, Rana heard the chatter and saw the flurry of activity. Carts packed, food stored. Word had come down from Moses and his brother, Aaron. The Hebrews would soon be on the move again.

"They say we must conserve our supplies." A woman with white hair and rheumy eyes grabbed hold of Rana's arm to tell her the news. "No one is sure how long it will take to cross the wilderness."

Just hours before, Rana had found a cozy bed outside the tent of a brickmaker, his wife, and their seven children. The children were careless, as children so often are, and the one named Caleb, who had been given the task, had not collected all the blankets that had been put out to air in the sun. She had slept well thanks to that forgotten blanket, at least for a few hours before the camp came alive, and she was in a better mood than she had been when she returned from the Red Sea with the donkey. If she were not so well rested, Rana might have told the woman with the rheumy eyes she cared only about supplies she could thieve from the other travelers for her own use.

Instead, she simply smiled as if she appreciated the advice, and since there was a cluster of women gathered nearby, children racing and chasing around them, she slipped into the group, the better to avoid further interaction. The women stood in a circle, their waterskins and baskets filled with bread and figs set in front of them, clucking like the hens that picked at the ground around their feet.

"Moses will lead us to the land God promised us," one woman said. "It is just on the other side of Shur I am told. We will be there soon."

A woman next to her lifted her lip. "But there is no water in Shur. Have you not heard the reports from the scouts? Has anyone bothered to mention that? I heard—"

"You listen to too many rumors, Chava," another woman told her. "Would Moses be taking us there if there was no water?"

"He nearly led us to our deaths at the Red Sea," Chava grumbled.

"Yet we were saved, were we not? God delivered His people." A woman with flashing eyes grabbed hold of a toddler who had stumbled and nearly fallen, and at the same time she settled the child back on her feet, she gave Chava a keen look. "You need to listen to our leaders more and pay less attention to those who are discontent and grumble against them."

Another child dashed by and bumped into Chava. When she spoke again, her words were as sharp as the swat on the rump she gave the little boy. "Perhaps, Tirzah, it would do no harm to listen to those who have other opinions, other plans. If we wander off blindly into the wilderness—"

"How can we be blind when we have our God to guide us?"

"How do we know it is God who is guiding us? Moses—"

"Delivered us from Egypt," Tirzah reminded her, her shoulders steady and her chin high.

Chava, too, raised her chin. "Then explain to me—"

"Explain something to all of us, Chava," another, younger woman called out. "Tell us how you came to have that beautiful bracelet you wear." She laughed, clearly trying to lighten the mood. "That is not a bauble for a slave girl."

Chava's hand went to the bracelet that dangled from her left wrist, and Rana looked that way. Even from where she stood at the back of the crowd of women, she could see the bracelet was finely made. Gold beads winked in the sunlight. They were intermingled with turquoise, bluer even than the sky, and carnelian, as red as blood. She thought back to Pithom and what that toad, Zoser, would say if she brought him such a prize.

"As valuable as three horses."

"The bracelet belonged to the woman I served." Chava's voice snapped Rana from her thoughts, though it did not make her look away. Her gaze stayed on the bracelet, the way it flashed and sparkled. "Let her sit now in her fine house and think about where the bauble has gone. Let her picture me wearing it. She is all alone now without her slaves around her to do her bidding. I hope she is as miserable as we were when we served her."

"Not a kind thought," one of the women scolded.

Chava tossed her head. "She was not a kind mistress. I have the scars on my back from her punishment rod to prove it."

"All the more reason you should be willing to follow those who teach us there are better ways to live," Tirzah told her. "We must listen to Moses and Aaron. They know far more about crossing the wilderness than we do. It is not the first time Moses has been out of Egypt, after all. He was a shepherd in Midian for many years. He knows what he is doing. We need to trust him, and our God. They know what glories await us in the Promised Land."

The only glory Rana cared about was the golden bracelet, and not simply because it was beautiful. In their journey to this Promised Land the Hebrews talked about, they were bound to encounter other travelers, tribesmen, and traders. If she could barter with such a bauble, she might win herself a place on a caravan back to Egypt.

"Moses knows the country around us is harsh," a woman said, and Rana didn't bother to look to see who was speaking. Skirting around the women, she closed in on Chava. And her bracelet. "That is why we have been told to be careful with our food and water."

"Careful?" As she stomped over to the nearest waterskin, Chava's voice was sharp. "I will show you what I think of being careful!" Chava pushed up the sleeves of her tunic. She removed her headscarf. She—though she saw it with her own eyes, Rana could not believe her luck—stripped off the bracelet and dropped it to the ground then reached for an earthen bowl that sat nearby, filled it, and poured the water over her head.

A thief knows when the gods smile on her, and after a whispered prayer of thanksgiving to Shai, the god of good fortune, Rana took full advantage of the situation. While some of the women berated Chava for being rash, others rushed forward to stop her from wasting any more of the precious water. In the chaos, Rana crept closer, and when a woman with a broad nose and a scar on her right cheek struck Chava on the arm and Chava fought back, swinging the earthenware bowl, Rana took full advantage of the confusion.

Slipping between a woman tugging at Chava's tunic and one trying to seize the waterskin to get it out of Chava's reach, Rana stooped, snatched up the bracelet, and tucked it into her palm. She knew better than to run and attract attention, so instead, she pretended to take part in the melee. She poked a short, round woman with her elbow and tromped on another's feet, all the while making her way to the perimeter of the crowd, waiting for the right moment to disappear. When Tirzah clapped her hands together and called out to the women to stop behaving like Egyptian street urchins, Rana supposed she could have been offended. Instead, she went on the alert. Things were bound to settle down. When the women stepped away from each other, breathing hard, pinning each other with narrow-eyed looks, she tensed. And when Chava grunted and reached for her headscarf then scanned the ground for her bracelet, Rana knew she had no more time to spare.

She whirled around, prepared to disappear into the throng that had gathered to watch the commotion. She might have made it more than a cubit's length if Gideon wasn't standing right behind her.

"Ah, the donkey woman." He looked down at her, his lips lifted into a smile that did not reflect in his eyes. "I might have known I would find you at the center of the trouble."

"But I am not, am I?" Rana lifted her shoulders, the picture of innocence. "These other women quarrel. I am just passing by."

"Just?" He looked her up and down.

She met his gaze, her own eyes steady, her voice containing the same hint of accusation as his. "Are you following me?"

"I happened to be…how did you put it? Just passing by."

"It is such a large camp, that seems unlikely."

He shrugged. "Yet at least in my case, it is true."

She stepped to the side. "Then I will let you continue on your way. Unless you are here to bedevil these poor women."

He laughed. It was a deep, warm laugh that made Rana think Gideon might not be as intimidating as he appeared. At least until he fixed her with an unwavering gaze. "It is foolish of Chava to waste water, but it is not my business to tell her so. She will find out for herself when she and her family get thirsty enough. No, I was not talking about that. What I meant is that these poor women will be bothered enough when they discover what you have done."

Her heart skipped a beat, and before she could remind herself that it was dangerous to react and risk giving away her secrets, she tightened her hold on the bracelet. "Done? The only thing I have done is stopped to chat."

He pursed his lips and his mustache bristled. "Odd, since I have never seen you chat with anyone."

"Ah, that proves it then! You have been following me."

A muscle twitched at the base of his jaw. "Merely observing. And the time or two I have seen you—"

"Because you were following me."

"Because I happened to notice you as I went about my duties." He bit the words in two, caught himself on the edge of losing his temper, and drew in a breath. "Part of my service to Joshua includes keeping an eye on things, assuring everyone's safety. And in doing that, I walk the camp. I talk to people."

"Surely not about me." Would he see how false her smile was? How it wavered around the edges? She added a laugh she hoped would distract him. "I cannot imagine what anyone would have to say."

"Which is curious, don't you think? Because I have asked people. And no one knows you. No one. Not even Micah, and he happens to own a donkey he was surprised to find laden down with waterskins this morning. Waterskins that were not there when he bedded down the donkey last night."

"Micah is old and forgetful." Rana hoped she was right.

"He might be old, but he has the eyesight of an eagle."

"Then perhaps you did not describe me accurately."

Gideon gave this some thought. "Too thin," he finally said, with another penetrating look at her. "Too brash. Quick, but perhaps…" Chava was now frantically searching the ground for her bracelet, and Gideon's gaze wandered to her before it drifted back to Rana. "Perhaps in this case, not quick enough. How am I doing so far?"

She pouted. "I am hardly brash. And how would you know, anyway? And even if you did, even if that is what you told Micah about me, well, he would not know that much about me. He merely asked me to take his donkey and use it to bring back the filled waterskins. If he does not even know what I look like—"

"I described you accurately, I think. Eyes like midnight on the Nile. A small nose, upturned at the end. Hair the color of the shadows."

His voice was soft, like a secret, and at the same time as it spread warmth through her, she had no choice but to dismiss what he said with a laugh. "All that and still Micah did not recognize me?"

"I told him you were shorter than me by at least a head, and that your left arm..." His gaze traveled that way, and since it was the hand in which she held the bracelet, she automatically tucked it beneath the folds of her tunic. "There is no use trying to hide it. I have already seen it. You have an ugly scar on your left wrist."

"You cannot have noticed that."

His smile came and went. "Childhood accident?"

A market merchant with a knife who wasn't happy to find her hand in a basket of his bread.

The memory made her wince, so as she always did, she refused to consider it.

"Micah did not know your name. Neither do I."

"I really must be going," she said, and she thought he'd let her.

That is, until he spoke so quietly, she wasn't sure she heard him. "I saw you take something."

It was impossible to pretend to be as brash as he believed she was when his eyes were on her, assessing, judging. Rana swallowed hard. "Did you? Where? When?"

"Just now. Here."

"From these women? What do they have worth taking?"

"Exactly what I was wondering." He moved a step closer. "If there was talk of something valuable among the women, I passed by too late to hear it." He pursed his lips as if he had to think about it, but Rana knew he didn't. She could tell Gideon was a man who knew his own mind. "I should talk to them. What do you say? I am sure they can tell me if anything of worth is missing."

Rana took a step back, closer to where the women were still milling about, gathering their children, shooing their chickens, grumbling about the foolishness of wasting water. At the center of it all was Chava, who kicked at the dirt. When she found nothing, her expression, so defiant such a short time before, melted. Confusion one second. Panic the next.

"You are mistaken," Rana told Gideon, at the same time she was bumped from behind by a woman heavy with child. She offered a quick smile to acknowledge the woman's apology and took the opportunity to slip closer to Chava. Another woman, this one with a baby propped on her hip, stepped between Rana and Gideon, and in that moment when he couldn't see her, Rana called on a simple trick she'd learned from a withered magician in the marketplace in Pithom. She deftly transferred the bracelet from her left hand to her right, put her right hand to her side, and dropped the bracelet on the ground. She had already stepped away when Chava, finally seeing the prize she was seeking, whooped with triumph.

Gideon couldn't prove a thing, and when she walked away, her chin high, Rana gave him a smile to tell him she knew it.

That smile didn't last long. "Son of a swine," she grumbled once she was well out of Gideon's earshot. "The bracelet was my prize, and I will never have another opportunity at it." She clenched her jaw and spoke to herself from between gritted teeth. "Gideon, you owe me. And since you will never pay me back for what I have lost…" She shot a look over her shoulder, but Gideon was no longer there.

"I will find another prize to cheer me," she told herself even though she knew that no matter what it was, it would not be as beautiful or as valuable as the bracelet.

Angry and determined, Rana made her way farther from the gaggle of women, deeper into the heart of the camp. She passed a pen filled with sheep where the young boy left to tend them dozed in the sun, a woman at her loom, her fingers moving like lightning over the cloth she made, an old man stacking pottery, wrapping it in cloths to protect it for the next day's journey. Nothing she saw was worth taking, and her mood soured even further. She would have kept right on walking if she hadn't caught the scent of freshly baked bread.

Rana's stomach rumbled, reminding her that the only thing she'd eaten that day was four small dates that had fallen from a woman's basket unnoticed. She followed the delicious aroma of the bread through a maze of tents and sheep pens. When she found its source, she bemoaned her luck. There was no newly baked bread stacked in a place where she might take it. This bread was still cooking on heated stones over the fire outside a tent with a blue curtain covering its doorway. Rana looked from her left to her right. There was no one around to stop her, but the bread looked as if it had just been put on the cooking stones. Even if she could manage to snatch some of it, it would be inedible.

Yet she wondered what other sorts of things might be found there. She called out to anyone inside the tent. When she got no answer, she dared to look through the goods left on a long woolen rug just outside the doorway. An iron comb. A basket filled with unspun wool piled in mounds as fluffy as clouds. Another basket of finished wool, evenly spun.

There was nothing there she could eat and nothing valuable enough to make it worthwhile to take the chance of getting caught stealing it. That is, until a flash of color from inside the tent caught her eye.

She dared to dart inside, and there, between a rug used as a bed and a mound of unspun wool, was a scarf much like the simple one she herself had stolen and wore so that she could more easily blend in with the Hebrews. This scarf, though, was nothing like hers, plain and roughly woven. This one was woven in colorful stripes, ochre and red, and a thin band of blue, and when Rana took it into her hands, the scarf felt soft against her skin, as smooth as the skin of an Egyptian noblewoman who adorns her body with milk and honey and almond oil. She tucked the scarf into her tunic and slipped from the tent.

It was her bad luck that just as she did, two women approached.

"Leah, look!" The woman on the left was thin and withered and had the face of a vulture, lean and long. She held out an arm and pointed a talon in Rana's direction. "That girl has come from inside your tent. And see there, she has your pretty scarf hidden in her tunic."

Hidden. But not hidden well enough. Rana chided herself. One corner of the scarf peeked from her neckline, the blue and ochre and red betraying her as surely as if she had plucked the scarf from her tunic and waved it in front of the women.

"Leah!" Because Leah hadn't moved, the vulture woman grabbed her sleeve and pulled her closer to the tent, and her voice was so loud, people gathered around to see what was happening. "Did you hear me? Do you see it? That girl was in your tent. She has stolen from you. You must do something about this. Now!"

Leah was shorter than Vulture Woman, rounder. She had large dark eyes, and underneath the headscarf she wore—one as simple as the one on Rana's head—her dark hair was speckled with white. She shrugged out of her friend's grasp and closed in, her head cocked, studying Rana. Rana and the scarf.

Vulture Woman scurried to stand behind her, her cheeks bright with the excitement of catching a thief. She waved an arm toward the people who now encircled the tent, cutting off any hope of escape. "One of you men, come quickly. Apprehend her!" she shouted. "One of you others, fetch Aaron, and then this girl's crime will be known to all. Leah, do not just stand there. What are you going to do about it?"

CHAPTER FOUR

Rana's stomach clenched. Her throat closed. For nothing more than a pretty headscarf, she had taken a foolish risk. It was reckless, and stupid of her not to think that sooner or later, she would be discovered for what she was, nothing more than an Egyptian stowaway, a thief who had dared to join the Hebrew exodus. Now she would be flogged. Or worse.

She was trapped. And it was impossible to escape. All because she'd been seduced by the scent of fresh bread.

As if Leah knew the thoughts that were passing through Rana's head, she sniffed and, realizing that the bread she'd left to cook would burn at any moment, hurried to the fire. She removed the bread from the cooking stones, blowing on her fingers when she set each piece down. Finished, she scraped her hands against her tunic and piled the bread onto a clay platter. On her way to the tent, she stopped—the plate of bread between her and Rana—and again, she glanced at the scarf that peeked from Rana's neckline.

In those few moments, Rana had a chance to study Leah. Her face was soft and round, and except for the wrinkles at the corners of her eyes, her skin was as smooth as the Nile on a sunny day. But those furrows near her eyes, they reminded Rana of the wadis they'd seen in their travels in the wilderness. Deep folds. Dry as the air that scraped their skin and parched their animals. They were large eyes, and brown. So like those of all the people Rana had met in the course of her life.

And yet something about them was so different.

There was an emotion that simmered in them, though Rana could not say what it was. Was the spark in Leah's dark eyes a warning of what was to come? Perhaps Leah was considering doling out Rana's punishment herself, or maybe she was thinking she might ask her vulture-faced friend to do it for her. The way Vulture Woman ran her tongue over her lips told Rana she would enjoy every minute of it. Or maybe the look in Leah's eyes meant she was considering calling someone else to assist her with the justice Rana deserved, someone like Gideon, who would drag Rana away, banish her from the camp, leave her in the wilderness with the snakes and the scorpions, the unrelenting sun and a powerful thirst.

A second passed, two, before Rana felt a shift in the air. Leah had made up her mind and, waiting, Rana tensed.

"My colorful scarf, did you say?" When she looked toward Vulture Woman, Leah's voice was as light as if they were discussing nothing more important than the latest camp gossip. "I think you are confused, Batya. I do not know what you are talking about."

Batya sputtered. "But you must," she insisted. "You must see it. There." She pointed at the scarf.

"Hmm." Leah considered this. But only for a moment before she angled her head toward the tent. "Come, girl," she said to Rana. "Come inside."

Without waiting to see if Rana would follow, Leah pushed aside the blue curtain and went into the tent. After she was gone, the curtain fluttering in her wake, Rana stood as still as the statue she had once seen of the lion-headed goddess Sekhmet, whose name means She Who is Powerful.

Rana wished she could feel but a bit of that power now so that she would have the courage to run away, to hide as she'd done all the days of their journey. But instead, an unfamiliar feeling flooded her, one that whispered to her in a voice she had never heard before. It told her that just this once, she should not give in to her baser instincts, the ones that urged her to fight. Just this once, the voice advised, she needed to follow another path, to be led by her heart.

And yes, her stomach too!

Without another look at Batya, Rana swept aside the blue curtain and stepped into the tent.

When she darted inside earlier in search of whatever treasure she could find, she hadn't had the luxury of looking around. Now she paused, letting her eyes adjust to the shadowed light inside, and saw that Leah's tent was small and as simple as the other tents she'd seen in the camp. Just blankets—and mismatched ones at that—tied and held up by wooden poles. Yet even in the middle of the wasteland where they found themselves, it was snug and welcoming, and it smelled sweet and grassy. There were rugs laid over the dusty ground, baskets in the corners that no doubt contained whatever worldly goods Leah was able to bring out of Egypt. The tent was filled with soft shadows, and it felt comfortable, like the kind of home Rana only imagined in her dreams.

Leah stood with her back to the doorway, her hands busy over something Rana couldn't see, and when she turned, she waved toward the largest of the rugs.

"Sit, sit. Set aside any bits and pieces of wool that might be in your way."

There were mounds of fluffy wool here and there, and Rana did as she was told, brushing them aside and making a place for herself.

Leah clicked her tongue. "The wool, it flies everywhere when I comb it. You would think by now, I would know better. I should work outside so things in here do not get so messy. I usually do. But it was so hot yesterday, was it not? More and more lately, I find it difficult to work in the heat. I need the coolness of my home."

Home.

It was so in line with what Rana had been thinking, she shivered, and again, she glanced around. "Is it?" she asked Leah. "Do you think of this as your home?"

The older woman nodded. "It is my home. For now. Until we get to the Promised Land."

"And then?" Rana wanted to know.

"Then we will settle. And worship the One True God. And be free. It is what our Lord God wants for us, I am sure you know that. It is why He led us out of Egypt."

Rana thought back on everything she'd seen, everything she'd heard talked about in the camp. "But it was Moses, wasn't it, who led the exodus?"

"Moses listened to God's word and did all God told him to do." She smiled. "Moses secured our freedom from Pharaoh, yes, but it was God who led him, every step of the way."

"Just as He did at the Red Sea." Rana could not help it. The memory of broken chariots and floating bodies still roiled her stomach.

Perhaps Leah knew it. Her smile softened. "Our God protects us. He defends us. He is our strength and our song. He has become our salvation. You heard Miriam and the other women singing those words when we first arrived here, did you not?"

Rana nodded.

"Miriam is the sister of Moses and Aaron. She knows our God's greatness, as we all do."

Leah held out a plate to Rana, a look in her eyes that reminded Rana of the time she'd seen an old man trying to coax a pup away from the river where a crocodile floated nearby. There were two pieces of bread on it along with some oil for dipping.

As tempting as it was, Rana did not dare reach for the bread. "You would share your food with me?"

Leah poked the plate at her. "Why would I not? If I know anything about people—and I have been told I am an excellent judge of character—it has been some time since you have had a full stomach." She offered the plate again. "Do you want it or not?"

Rana did not wait to be asked again. She snatched the plate from Leah's hands. The aroma of the bread filled her nostrils. Her mouth watered. She'd already bitten into the bread, chewed, swallowed, and sighed before she realized it was not the way a guest in someone else's home acted. Fire heated Rana's cheeks, but before she could stammer an apology, Leah waved a hand.

"No need." Leah took a plate of bread for herself and sat on the rug opposite Rana. "We thank God for what He has given us, do we not? I believe that He, in turn, is pleased that we take pleasure from His gifts. From the look on your face, I would say God is very pleased with you."

It was on the tip of Rana's tongue to insist that could not be true. Even if she believed in the Hebrew God, she did not think He could be happy with an orphan thief. She might have pointed this out if she wasn't so busy dipping the bread in the oil and taking another bite.

"It is very good." Rana sopped up what remained of the oil with the last of her bread. Before she even finished swallowing it, Leah offered another piece.

Rana gladly accepted it. "You have made all this wonderful bread? Just for yourself?"

Leah shrugged. "As I am sure you know, it takes a great deal of work to make bread. Hours of grinding grain. More time to mix the dough with water." She shrugged off the thought of the effort. "If I am making some, I might as well make more. Besides, I never know who might appear outside my tent. You are living proof of that, no?" She smiled but didn't wait for Rana to answer. "My neighbors around here…" She glanced toward the doorway. "Some of them are hungry too. They did not all pack sufficient supplies for the journey."

Rana thought back to all she'd heard on the streets of Pithom about Moses and the plagues his God brought down on Egypt. About his demands that Pharaoh free the Hebrews. About Pharaoh's stubbornness, his refusal. Until the night death passed over Egypt and Pharaoh changed his mind.

"How is it you were so well prepared?" Rana asked. "You could not have had any more warning than anyone else did that you—"

She caught herself and smothered the word in another mouthful of bread and did not speak again until she'd swallowed it. "You could not have known that we were leaving. No one knew."

"But we all knew, didn't we?" Leah did not say this as a challenge. Her voice was as soft as the faraway look in her eyes. "Our God promised He would deliver us."

"And you believed this? What, even when the Hebrews were slaves?"

Leah's laugh was warm. "Especially when we were slaves. God is good. And He is powerful. He loves His people. He would not let them suffer forever. And now…" She pulled in a deep breath and let it out slowly. "It is a new life, a new beginning. For all of us." Her gaze drifted to Rana's empty plate. "One more piece?"

"One more piece." Rana held out her plate, and Leah deposited a disk of bread on it.

"Now tell me," Leah said. "Where is your family?"

The bread stuck in Rana's throat.

"Ah," was all Leah said when Rana didn't answer. "So many families were torn apart when we were slaves. That does not mean you cannot find yours again. Your people must be here in the camp. What are their names?"

Rana was saved from answering when the curtain on the doorway was pulled aside.

"Leah! Leah! What is happening in there?" Batya marched into the tent, and with the curtain open, Rana saw a group of people gathered outside, craning their necks to see what was going on. "We are worried for your safety," Batya said, though to Rana's way of thinking, with their eyes bright and their expressions eager,

Batya and her friends looked more like they didn't want to miss out on anything. "You are in here with a stranger, Leah. With a thief! I had to be certain there was nothing bad going on. Are you all right?"

Leah, it seemed, was not one to get riled. Even under such questioning. She didn't rise, simply waved a hand toward the plates of bread. "We are sharing a meal," she said, as if Batya and her prying friends could not see that for themselves. "We are talking. And sharing a meal. Maybe you would like to join us?" She scooted over on the rug to make room for Batya and anyone else who might take up the invitation.

No one did, and it was no wonder why.

"Break bread with a thief?" Batya's words were sharp, her top lip curled. "I would sooner starve in the wilderness."

Batya's words were echoed by the people wedged into the doorway behind her.

"Yes."

"Starve."

Leah laughed. "Then go ahead and starve." She shooed them away as if they were nothing more than a swarm of mosquitoes. "We are enjoying our bread and getting to know each other."

Rana didn't catch what Batya said when she dropped the curtain and left, but she did hear the grumble of disapproval from outside. "Perhaps I should go," Rana said.

"Do not be silly. Batya and her kind are always looking to stir up trouble. She was no different in Egypt. You would think freedom would have sweetened her disposition. Pay her no mind. I meant what I said. If she and her friends do not like what I do and who I eat with, they can just go on their way. It is none of their business. Except…" There was just a bit of bread left on Leah's plate, and she pinched it between thumb and forefinger and nibbled it. "I was not exactly honest with them, was I? Because I said we were getting to know each other and that is not exactly true." Her look was gentle, but probing. "You have not even told me your name."

"Does it matter, do you suppose?"

Leah leaned forward, took the empty plate from Rana's hands, and stood to carry it away. "Yes, it matters. We all matter to each other. We are all children of the same God."

"But in Egypt—" Rana swallowed the rest of her words. She'd been so close to letting the words slip and telling Leah that in Egypt, no one cared enough about an outcast to ask her name. Imagine that! A few pieces of bread. A little oil. Leah's smile. And she nearly let down the walls around her heart that had taken a lifetime to build. She had nearly told her secret. She reprimanded herself for such weakness and swore it would not happen again.

To calm herself, Rana scooped up a handful of wool that had been left on the rug. It was the color of goat's milk, as downy as a cloud, and she ran it through her fingers. Too late, she found out it prickled.

She didn't even realize she'd made a face until Leah laughed. "Unspun wool. By the time it is washed and woven and we are wearing it on our backs, we forget that when it comes from the sheep, it needs a great deal of work and care."

"Is that what you do?"

There was an odd instrument on the floor near Leah, and she picked it up and showed it to Rana. "I am a spinner, yes. As was my mother and her mother before her. This is one of the spindles I use to twist the wool into the long threads the weaver uses at her loom. And this…" She reached for the iron comb Rana had seen when she came into the tent the first time. "This is a comb I use to clean the wool when it first comes from the sheep. The wool can contain briars and other dirt that has to be gotten rid of."

"It must take a great deal of time."

"It does. But it is satisfying work. After all, our people are the only ones who use wool for clothing." Leah's eyes drifted to Rana's tunic. "The Egyptians say sheep and goats are filthy animals, and they won't use their fleece. They wear only linen. It is too bad for them. They are missing out on the wonderful properties of wool. As I am sure you know, it keeps us warm at night, and it can protect against rain too. In Egypt, I spun linen for my master all day long. Then when I got back to my quarters in Goshen, I would spin wool for our people far into the night. It was an honor."

"So much work, and you do it all by yourself?" It was an insolent question, yet Rana did not excuse herself. It was only natural she'd be curious.

"Not all of it, of course." Leah laughed. "It takes an army of women to spin enough to clothe all of the people of the twelve tribes. But I do a great deal of it." She turned her back on Rana, and her voice was muffled. "Now I do it myself. But it was not always so."

"You had helpers."

Leah turned. The sun had moved in the sky, and the light was dimmer. It shadowed Leah's face and added a wash of gray that took the sparkle from her eyes. "I had a daughter," she said.

"And was she a spinner too?"

"The finest spinner I have ever seen. And I do not say that simply because I was her mother." Leah's sigh rippled the air. "Oh, how her fingers could fly over the fleece. It had always been so, ever since she first started helping me when she was a child. I suppose it was in our blood, but Eliana, she had a special gift. Her fingers were so nimble. Her eye was so good. And her touch! She knew exactly how much to twist the fiber. It was never too tight, never too loose. She created a little miracle every time she sat down with her spindle. Threads as soft as a baby's cheek, as fine as a summer breeze. My own yarn?" Leah gave a muffled laugh. "It is good enough. And it has clothed many a man, woman, and child. But Eliana's was special. When it was dyed, it soaked in the colors. They were so wondrous and true."

Rana glanced down at the bit of scarf tucked into her tunic. Red. And ochre. And a glorious blue like the sky about the sacred Nile.

"Did she…" Rana thought it best to change the subject. "Did Eliana spin linen for the Egyptians too?"

Leah nodded. "It was her Egyptian mistress who…" Her voice caught. "Eliana had not been feeling well, and she was not spinning as fast as her mistress thought she should be. The woman took a rod to Eliana."

From the look on Leah's face, Rana knew the story did not have a happy ending. "The master killed your Eliana?"

Leah shook her head. "She was gravely injured. She came home to me, and she lingered for three days. Then finally…" She drew in a long breath and let it out again slowly. "Eliana, she often spoke of the joy of being free and in the Promised Land. She would be happy to be with us. Then again, as long as I have some of her work, she is with me." Leah shook her shoulders. "Now, I have told you something about myself and my life in Egypt. Tell me, girl, what did you do there?"

"I worked at the marketplace," Rana said, and really, it wasn't a lie. She often went to the market to see what goods she could snatch.

Leah could not have known that. She considered this and nodded with satisfaction. "Helping at a market stall, that seems an easier job than some slaves had. They were kind to you?"

"Kind?" Rana rolled the word over her tongue. She could not remember a time she'd seen kindness. Not until she walked into Leah's tent.

The thought caused a funny feeling to bunch between her heart and her stomach, and rather than consider it and all it might mean, she scrambled to her feet. "I have taken up enough of your time," she told Leah. "We are leaving tomorrow, you know."

"And I must spend the rest of the day packing away my belongings." Leah grabbed for some fleece and bunched it in her hand. "I will sit outside and spin for a while first. It helps ease my heart to spin after I talk of Eliana. You may stay if you wish."

"No. Really." Rana backed toward the doorway, and when she did, her foot caught on the edge of the rug and she fell to her knees. Her tunic pulled up, and though she hopped to her feet again as quickly as she could and tugged it back into place, there was no doubt Leah had seen the linen sheath she wore under it.

It was one thing to be known as a thief. It was another altogether to be found out to be an Egyptian, an enemy of the Hebrew people and the God who struck down those who opposed them. Rana would get no further kindness from Leah. She knew that now for certain. She swept aside the blue curtain and hurried outside.

Leah stayed in the tent. Batya and her friends, thankfully, were nowhere to be seen. Rana was alone again as she had always been.

It was time for her to again melt into the anonymity of the camp, but before she did, she plucked Eliana's beautiful scarf from her tunic and left it in Leah's doorway.

CHAPTER FIVE

The Wilderness of Shur was a most unwelcoming place, and after just one day of traveling there, Rana wished she knew when they might get to the other side, to wherever it was Moses was leading them. She couldn't wait for the journey to be over. The same sun, the light of Ra, beat down on Pithom as it did here in the middle of nowhere, but in Pithom, at least, there were the shadows of buildings to cool off in, and the occasional tradesman or traveler in the taverns who, in exchange for her sham of a smile and the interest she pretended as he droned on and on about himself, would offer her a beer to quench her thirst.

Unlike the streets of Pithom, here the land was pitted and rocky, and she'd lost count of how many times that day she'd turned her ankles. In Pithom, when the moon was at its darkest and the city slept, she would sometimes steal onto the grounds of a lavish home and cool off in the pools of water filled and refilled by the house slaves for the pleasure of their masters. In Shur, the air was as dry as the dust kicked up by the Hebrews and their beasts. It scoured Rana's skin. It gritted between her teeth. It stuck in her throat, and more than once during that long day, she slipped from one group to the next, searching for whatever water she could find, and when she did, she gulped it like a drunkard.

No matter how much she drank, it never seemed enough, and by nightfall, though she was bone-tired from walking, it was clear she wouldn't sleep. Not when her tongue was stuck to the roof of her mouth and her face was coated with grime. When the Hebrews made camp, she took the opportunity to blend in with a group of stone carvers who had gathered their carts in a circle around a sputtering fire. They were far from the blazing pillar that hovered at the center of the camp, and to Rana's way of thinking, that was perfect. If the stone carvers could not see her clearly, they wouldn't discover she was a stranger.

She sat herself in the shadows between a man with a twisted right arm and a woman who held a squirming baby. When those in the group passed a cup of water, person to person, and praised their God for all He provided them, she waited, parched and impatient. When the cup finally came to her, Rana forced herself to sip, not guzzle, but she did make sure she dribbled enough water on her chin so that she could dab the droplets to the back of her neck.

Again, the memory of Pithom crashed over her. Those stolen nights in pools where she had no business, dipping her head beneath the cool water and leaping upright again so that the water cascaded down her neck and caressed her arms. She was surprised when her heart squeezed and her eyes welled. She had never felt such yearning. More than ever, she wished she could be back in Egypt.

For now, she would have to content herself with one more small sip of water. Then, as the others had done, she passed the cup to the person seated on her left, and since it was nearly empty, the man with the twisted arm got up to fill it from a nearby waterskin. On his way back to rejoin the circle, he made a face.

"I am puzzled," he said. "There is little water left in the skin."

"That is impossible," the woman to the other side of him whined. "Or at least it would be if you did as you were supposed to do. I told you, Jacob, at the last well we passed. I told you to fill the skins completely. If you listened to me—"

"How can I not listen to you, Devorah?" Jacob rolled his eyes. "You never stop talking!"

"And you never once do what I tell you to do," Devorah grumbled. "We should have more than enough water."

"We did have more than enough," Jacob insisted. "I saw to it myself. Yet now, the skins are so much lighter than they should be. Unless one of you..." He glanced around the circle, his eyes flashing with the reflected light of the fire, his voice edged with accusation. "We all decided. Before we left Goshen. We said that among us, we would share our water and our food supplies equally. If one of you has taken more than you should, then—"

"Are you saying one of us has been using too much water?" The woman with the baby threw back her head and snorted. "The skins have been in your cart all day, Jacob. Maybe it is you and Devorah we should be asking about where the water has gone."

"Bah!" Jacob tossed back a mouthful of water and passed the cup on. "You know how careful I have been. You have seen it yourself a dozen times today."

"Yes, when you would not let us have even a sip of water," a man grumbled. "Not even when we stopped to rest."

"We do not know how long it will be until we reach the next wells," Jacob pointed out. "If it is days—"

"Do we have enough water for days?" an old man with a scraggly white beard wanted to know.

"Yes, yes," Jacob insisted, but his gaze snaked back to the waterskins beyond the circle of the fire's light. "We have enough."

Jacob, it seemed, was not much of a liar. Rana was sure. For one thing, he looked away from the old man when he spoke. For another, as a skilled liar herself, she knew a fraud when she saw one. Jacob, Devorah, and the stonemasons did not have enough water.

And she had no wish to waste her time in a place where there was nothing to be gained.

As quietly as she could, Rana slipped away from the circle, but it was not so easy to leave her worries behind. Was the water supply running low? Throughout the camp? Or were stonemasons simply lazy men who had not done all the work required to ensure an adequate supply? Were their wives wasteful when they washed up? Were their children careless? Did they spill precious water when they filled their cups? She thought back to Chava, the woman with the beautiful bracelet, who had poured water over her head as recklessly as if she were standing on the banks of the sacred Nile and it was hers in endless measure.

There is no use worrying about it, she told herself. But it was not so easy to shove the thought from her mind, even when she finally found a place to sleep that night, wedged between a cart and an outcropping of rocks. And harder still not to tell herself that someday, she would have all the water she needed.

If only she could find her way back to Egypt.

On their second day in Shur, Rana fell in with a group of girls who were so busy sharing stories and gossip, they barely noticed her. There were twelve of them, and in Egypt, they had all been servants in different households. While they shared experiences, they did not know each other, and that, Rana decided, was perfect for her purposes. Thanks to her knowing just enough to join in their conversation, they assumed that she, like they, had been a house slave and accepted her without question.

They talked of the clothing and jewelry the guests wore and the perfumes they used that filled the air with the scents of frankincense and myrrh, cinnamon and honey. Eventually, their conversation turned from that to food.

One of the girls purred, "My favorite thing to eat is roasted quail."

"You had a taste of quail?" Another of the girls huffed in disbelief. "That is not possible. After all the work of serving a grand meal at the home where I was a slave, I was lucky to get even a crust of bread from my master."

"It is possible," the first girl assured her with a wink. "When you are friendly enough with the steward of the house."

The girls burst into laughter, and from there, the talk turned to men. Rana heard their opinions about who in the camp would make a suitable husband, and how lucky any girl would be to be chosen for marriage.

As the morning wore on and the sun rose higher in the sky, though, their chatter melted in the heat. Like the hundreds walking around them, they hoisted their packs on their backs, put their heads down, and trudged on. There was water at midday, shared by a man named Joseph, who had a broad nose and a wide smile, though even as she drank it, one of the girls grumbled that it was not as much as he had given them the day before. There was bread, but another girl was quick to point out, "Joseph's wife gave us three pieces each yesterday, and today, she says we must make do with two."

The bread, Rana thought, was not nearly as tasty as what she'd shared with Leah, but it would have to do. She comforted herself and her rumbling stomach with memories of Pithom, where in the shadow of the grain storehouses, there was plenty of food to steal.

By the morning of the third day in Shur, she was certain things could not get worse. She found out soon enough that she was wrong. The pitiless sun washed all color from the sky and made her eyes ache. Her skin roasted and blistered. That day she walked behind an old man and woman, their sons and daughters, their children, and their children's children. The old man fainted twice, and each time, his wife used a damp cloth against his forehead to revive him. Once he could finally move again, their oldest son commanded the others to take what few possessions they had from their cart and leave them in the dust so his father would not have to walk the rest of the way.

At this, the smallest of the children began to whine, and their high-pitched voices grated on Rana's nerves. She finally drifted from the group and fell in behind the men who were charged with finding the animals that had succumbed to the heat and thirst. One by one, a sheep here and a goat there, they loaded the carcasses onto carts for butchering at their next camping place.

Oftentimes, they were too late. The vultures that had been circling high above them all that day, black specks against the blinding sun, got to the animals first.

Eaters of the Dead.

Pharoah's Chickens.

Rana thought of the names she'd learned for the birds that were so sacred to her people that whoever dared harm one was sentenced to death. She had once seen a statue of Nekhbet, the goddess who had the body of a woman and the head of a vulture, and she thought of Nekhbet's long limbs and her white crown and how she looked so powerful, so beautiful and yet so terrifying. Nekhbet's vultures fed on death and assured rebirth. They carried remains from the earth into the skies above, and though Rana knew this to be true and reminded herself to be thankful for it and to praise Nekhbet for her service to mankind, she turned her head and hurried past when she saw one of her sacred birds pick the flesh from an unfortunate animal.

She found little water that night and even less the next morning, and by then, complaints rumbled through the camp like thunder.

"Moses should have told us."

"Moses did not prepare us properly."

"What has happened to the water? And the grain supplies. Why have they dwindled as well? That is what I would like to know."

"Do you think Moses and Aaron are suffering, eh, like we are? Do they have enough food and water for themselves and their families?"

They did not have long to complain. The pillar changed from fire to cloud, and they started off again. Another day in Shur.

By midday, Rana felt she couldn't move another step. Yet she kept on, and when she heard a hum all around her, her heat-addled brain convinced her it was nothing more than a bit of the fevered dream she'd been having, one about the Season of Inundation, when the Nile rose and watered the land, the breezes were cooler, and the smell of damp earth made the air heavy and fragrant with musk.

A second later, though, the man walking in front of her stopped abruptly and she jerked to awareness. It was then she realized the sound was no dream. All around her, the people spoke, their voices muffled at first then gaining strength, and after a while, the air all around her shivered with their excited words.

"There is a well up ahead!"

"Did you hear that?" A woman nearby turned and called to the people who followed behind them. "There is water nearby!"

Word passed person to person through the crowd, and soon the drone of their voices transformed into a song. The Hebrews thanked their God for His goodness and His protection, and they praised their leaders for their wisdom, their dusty voices suddenly filled with hope and the promise of satisfying their thirst. Women laughed and danced. Men raised their children on their shoulders and hurried forward. Rana didn't wait, not for the old people nearby who had to think about the good news and what they should do about it. Or the children who grabbed each other's hands and spun in circles. She darted around them. Slipped between their carts and their livestock. Weighted down so short a time ago by the heat and her worries, she felt as light as a feather now, racing forward until she was at the very front of the crowd. Ahead of her, a man stood atop a rocky outcropping. There was a stunted tree next to him, a smile on his face every bit as bright as the sun. The man waved an arm to get everyone's attention, and then he pointed down and yelled, "The well! Here it is. Here is water!"

She was not the first one to get to the water. That was an old man in a long white robe, and he only managed to get ahead of Rana because when he approached, the crowd parted and let him through. He stepped up to the well and motioned to the man who had come with him to drop a bucket into it. When the man pulled up the bucket, the old man's gray beard twitched.

He took the bucket in two hands and raised it to the sky.

"We thank our God," he said, and he took a long drink.

Then just as quickly spat the water out.

A gasp went through the crowd, and people cried out, "What is it? What is happening?"

"The water..." The man with the gray beard spat on the ground. "This water is bitter. No man or beast can drink it."

"What is that he said?" someone from the back of the crowd called out. "The water is no good?"

"The water is no good," someone repeated, and soon the whole of the crowd around Rana took up the words.

"The water is no good."

Rana's head told her the old man with the beard must surely know what he was talking about.

But her heart didn't believe it. Her dry mouth refused to listen. No god, Hebrew or Egyptian, could be so cruel to the people who worshiped him as to make them suffer from thirst.

She rushed forward, took the bucket in her hands, and gulped down a mouthful of the water.

Bitter.

Terrible.

She gagged and spit the water out then rubbed her mouth on the sleeve of her tunic. Even that wasn't enough to rid her of the horrible taste. Or the terrible truth of the situation. The Hebrews may have found the water they so desperately needed, but they would not be able to drink even a little of it.

Rana dropped the bucket. Where was the Hebrew God now? She wanted to demand an answer, but the people around her wouldn't have listened or heard. They stood with their shoulders drooped and their heads down, and some of them wept.

"It is not possible," a woman moaned. "Water is water. There can be no good water. No bad water."

When the woman stepped toward the well, a man put a hand on her arm. "It is true, *Imma*. We will find nothing here to quench our thirst."

"Are we surprised?" A man stepped forward. He was short and slight, and his eyes were small and set close to each other. Like a weasel's. "We knew what was going to happen, didn't we? We said it three days ago when we came into Shur."

"We said the water supply was low," someone yelled.

"We said there wasn't enough. Not for all of us."

"We said Moses has led us astray," a gruff voice added.

The crowd muttered its agreement, and it was that, Rana thought, that gave the short man the courage to climb the rocky outcrop. The man who'd pointed out the well stepped away, and the short man put his hands on his hips and looked all around.

"This proves we were right all along. We did not bring the proper supplies with us. We were not told how difficult this journey would be. Now it is time we came to our senses. Back in Egypt—"

"Back in Egypt, we were slaves," a man called out.

"Back in Egypt," the short man snapped, "we may have had to work hard, but we never had to worry about not having water to wet our tongues. Or food to fill our stomachs." He pointed to a man who stood near Rana. "Tell me, fellow, did you get enough to eat last night?"

"Well, no," the man answered. "But it is surely no one's fault. We did not bring as much grain as we should have."

"Or we should not have come into this wilderness at all," the short man said.

Another rumble went through the crowd.

"Were your Egyptian masters so cruel to you that they would deny you a drink?" His arm extended, his hand shaking, the man pointed, person to person. "Your mistress, the woman who owned the home where you toiled and gave you a place to put your head every night, did she ever say you should go to bed hungry? That you should crawl in the street, your mouth filled with sand and your body so overheated you could barely stand?"

"It happened," a man insisted. "I have seen it."

"Yes." The short man nodded. "A time or two. We all saw it a time or two in Pithom and in Raamses, Pharaoh's treasure cities. But not to many. Not to us. Or we would not be here, eh?"

"What are you saying?" someone demanded. "That our lives were better when we were slaves?"

"I think that may be true," a man called from somewhere back in the crowd. "I was never this miserable in Egypt. Not even when I was making bricks."

"That may be so," a woman called out, "but our God—"

"Our God has brought us to a place where the heat is burning our skin," the thin man pointed out. "He has delivered us from slavery and teased us with the promise of water. And here it is." He pointed down to the well. "Water we cannot drink!"

"It is true. It is true," a man called out.

"Then we must simply go on," a woman said. "We must continue and—"

Her advice was drowned by a chorus of disagreement.

A man with a bristling beard called out to the thin man on the rock. "What do you suggest we do?"

"Do?" he spat the word back. "There is only one thing we can do if we wish to stay alive. We must return to Egypt."

The very words made Rana's heart skip a beat. She looked around the crowd, eager to see who would object and, more importantly, who would agree.

A man bobbed his head.

A woman mumbled, "Yes, he is right. He is right. I never thought I would even think it, but yes, he is right."

And all around them, others took up the chorus.

The thin man lost no time in encouraging them. "Get your things together," he called, "those of you who are willing to go back to a place where at least we have the sustenance we need. Carts and animals." He pointed to his right, away from the well and the rocky outcropping. "Some of you get them organized over there. The rest of you, those who are not willing to be baked in the oven of the wilderness..." He jumped down from the rocks. "Follow me!"

He led the way, and Rana couldn't say how many people followed. She didn't stop to count. She fell in with the crowd, her footsteps suddenly lighter than they had been since the day she escaped the Medjay and joined the Hebrews. Her heart beat so hard with excitement, she thought it might burst from her chest.

They were going back. To Egypt. She didn't know how or what road they would follow, she only knew she would not be alone. She would soon see Pithom again.

But she was not fool enough to walk there.

A quick look around, and Rana slipped into the nearest cart and covered herself with some of the fabric piled there. With any luck, she could keep herself on the fringes of the group just as she'd done all the way through the wilderness, and once they were back in Pithom, the Hebrews might again be slaves, but she would be free.

She sighed with contentment and dug her shoulders into the soft fabric. With any luck, they would start out immediately.

"Good work." Close to the cart, she heard a man chuckle, accompanied by a slap, as if he'd given someone a reassuring pat. "You explained our predicament well."

"I did, didn't I?" Rana recognized the voice of the thin man who had convinced at least some of the Hebrews of the madness of what they were doing. "How many do you suppose will come back with us?"

She heard the other man make a noise, as if he was chewing on his bottom lip, counting the people she could hear milling around, organizing their possessions and their families for their return to

Egypt. "A few hundred at least," he finally said. "It is not all I would have liked."

"But it is a start," the thin man said.

"You think so?" This was a third man, a third voice, and though she could not place it, it seemed familiar to Rana, enough that it set off an alarm inside her that made her stomach knot. "It is a paltry number to return with. We need more of them. Many more."

"We tried," the thin man whined.

"Try harder," the third man rasped, his voice low and menacing, and Rana knew then why just hearing him speak made her tremble with fear.

It was Asim. The Medjay who, back in Pithom, had sworn he would kill her.

CHAPTER SIX

Rana's heart battered her ribs. Her stomach bunched. A scream built in her throat, and before it could escape and give away her hiding place, she pressed her fist to her mouth and dug her teeth into her knuckles. Better a little pain than taking the chance of being discovered.

Asim?

Here with the Hebrews?

She could not say how long she lay there. She only knew that with each passing second, panic built inside her until it pounded so hard in her blood, her head ached.

Back in Pithom, Asim said he would kill her if he ever saw her again, but once she joined the Hebrew caravan, she hadn't given him another thought. Now, she could not help but picture her last day in Pithom and the way he whipped his rod through the air when he spoke of her. She could not stop herself from thinking about the acid in his voice. If he was somehow here and with so many thousands of people milling about, moving, driving their animals, pitching and taking down their tents...

Rana bit her knuckles so hard, tears streamed down her cheeks.

Here in the wilderness, Asim was certain to find the chance to kill her. It would be easy enough for him to blend in with the other travelers, just as she'd done. And once the deed was done, it would be simple enough to dispose of her body in the vast emptiness.

No one knew her.

No one would miss her.

And even now, if she called out for help, she wondered if anyone would care enough to come running.

The thought of being alone and abandoned roused her instinct for self-preservation, and after a second, it sizzled like lightning through her. If no one else would save her, she would have to save herself. It was as simple as that. She needed a plan and a means of escape. She held her breath and listened, hoping Asim would speak again so she'd have some idea how much he knew about her comings and goings and how much time she had until he pounced on her.

But though she kept still and listened for a very long time, she heard nothing at all, and, realizing it, dared to take a breath. Her heartbeat settled, and something about the silence helped her head to clear.

Asim.

Here with the Hebrews.

She had let her imagination run away with her, imagining danger where there was none at all.

Asim?

Here with the Hebrews!

There was as little chance of that as there was of Rana herself ever entering the sacred temple of Ra and being welcomed there with gifts of gold and jewels by the pharaoh himself.

Asim was not a Hebrew. He wouldn't consort with them. And he wouldn't have followed her into the wilderness all the way from Pithom.

She was simply not worth it.

She was nothing. No one. A common thief. And a man as mighty and as important as Asim had better things to worry about than a thief.

It might actually be funny if it wasn't so pathetic to think that for a few heart-stopping minutes, she'd actually believed her life was in danger.

She did not need to remind herself that she never allowed herself to be frightened.

To prove it—to herself, to the world—Rana threw off the fabric that covered her and sat up in the cart, fully prepared to take stock of the men who'd been talking and prove to herself they were nothing more than Hebrews. Men, not the slaughterer demon, Asim, who haunted her nightmares.

But like the silence it had taken her a few moments to grasp, it took a few more moments to take in what she saw. Or rather, what she didn't.

There was no one anywhere nearby. Realizing it, the fear drained from Rana and left her feeling slack-kneed. Convinced her eyes must be playing tricks on her, she cautiously jumped from the cart and, one slow and careful step after another, she walked all around it, searching the area.

The thin man who'd called the Hebrews together and urged them to return to Egypt was nowhere to be seen. The discontented Hebrews who, in their hunger and thirst, feared for their lives and questioned their leaders' judgment, were not there either. Their animals had not been gathered. Their wives and children were not waiting. The rocky flatland where they had assembled their carts into the loose and disorganized caravan was deserted and as quiet as the houses of eternity where the mighty were entombed.

It wasn't until she looked across the camp that Rana saw why. There, where only a short while before the thin man had encouraged the Hebrews to rise up against Moses, a sea of people surged toward the bitter well and the rocky outcropping. There looked to be another man atop the rocks now, a man nearly as tall as the twisted tree. The sun shone full on him and blinded Rana so that it was impossible for her to see his face, but she could make out that he wore sandals and a simple tunic of undyed wool. Just another of the travelers.

And yet not so, for the host of Hebrews was drawn to him, quieter now than they had been when they called out in support of the thin man. Reverent. Respectful.

Rana moved closer, and though she could not clearly see the man's features, she saw the way his long gray beard jutted forward and showed he had a firm chin, as strong as the cornerstone of Pharaoh's palace.

Though she had heard no talk of the presence of such a being here in the Hebrew camp, she decided he must surely be a god, for no mere mortal could command the attention of thousands as he did. Men and women waited with anticipation, children stood at attention, and when he called out to all the people, his voice rumbled like thunder.

From this far away, it was difficult to understand what he said, and it was only natural she would move as close as she could to the outcropping and the man. When she did, she put a hand above her eyes to block the sun so that she could get a better look at him. His face was carved deep with wrinkles. His fingers were gnarled from hard labor. But his eyes... She sucked in a breath that was part awe, part wonder, and pure surprise. He had the kindest eyes of any man she'd ever seen, like a touch of evening starlight or the soft caress of a breeze on a hot day. After he looked all around at the people gathered around, he cried out to the God of the Hebrews, and his voice echoed through the stony wilderness. His words washed over them all. His voice made Rana's bones vibrate.

"Have you forgotten what we learned when we were slaves back in Egypt? Have you lost the wisdom won by our trials there? What about the plagues our God brought down on Egypt? Have they slipped your minds? Do you remember what they taught you? If you will diligently listen to the voice of the Lord your God, and if you will do that which is right in His sight and listen to His commandments and keep His laws, He promised to put none of the diseases on you that He brought down on the Egyptians. He has proved that to you, has He not?"

"Yes! Yes!" The people cried out in return.

"He brought death to the Egyptians," someone from the back of the crowd called out.

"And He passed over our houses," a man nearby shouted.

"And He gave us our freedom," a woman yelled.

"And by His power, Moses opened the Red Sea so we could pass through it," another said.

The man on the rocks listened and nodded. "He has done all these good things for us. Then why are you so foolish to lose your trust in Him? Why do you think He would abandon us now?" His words struck a chord. All around Rana, people hung their heads. Some wept, ashamed that they'd lost faith and hope.

The man went on. "The Lord says, 'I brought you out of Egypt. I am the Lord who heals you.' And yet all it takes for you to abandon Him is one taste of bitter water."

"We cannot drink our faith," a woman cried out, her voice defiant. "We cannot keep our children alive on promises."

Rana thought the man would take offense, but instead, he said, "Our God would never ask that of you. But what you can do…" He pivoted and looked at the crowd that, by now, was close upon every side of the rocky outcropping, hanging onto his every word. "Instead of abandoning your hope, instead of complaining to each other, cry out to the Lord to save you from the bitterness!"

"We do!" a man yelled. "We call out to our God who is our hope."

"Yes!" The people took up the call. "Yes! Yes!" And once the air was alive with it, the vibration of the word like a living thing against Rana's skin, the man turned to the tree that grew on the rocky ground above the bitter well. He wrapped his arms around the tree. He pulled. He grunted, took a deep breath, and pulled some more.

"This is madness, that is what it is," a woman near Rana grumbled. "The heat and thirst must have hurt his brain. What does he think he is doing?"

"No, no. Not mad," another woman said, shushing the first woman with a wave of her hand. "He is angry. Of course he is. He must have heard the way that other man spoke. How he urged people to leave here and return to Egypt. How some were willing to join him and go back. That is so disrespectful. He has every right to be infuriated. We should all feel the same."

"And he is taking his anger out on a tree?" a man scoffed. "That makes no sense at all."

It didn't, and it was exactly why Rana's insides jingled with anticipation. When she heard a crack like the sound of a rock breaking in two, her breath caught just as the tree swayed.

"He has ripped it from its roots." His voice filled with awe, a man who stood nearby pointed. "He has torn the tree from the earth."

He had, and a part of Rana wasn't surprised. She'd already decided the figure on the outcropping was a god. Of course he was able to do miraculous things. Yet watching him, she couldn't help but wonder, would a god wrench a tree from the earth and then be so red-faced? Would he gasp and pant as he hauled the tree to the edge of the outcropping?

"Do you think our Lord and God has abandoned you?" the man shouted to the crowd. His voice shivered against the rocks. "Do you doubt His love for His people?"

After what they had just seen, no one dared answer, and he didn't wait to see if they would. With a shout, he lifted the tree on his shoulder and pitched it into the bitter well.

Like the waves Rana had seen on the Red Sea, water rose and splashed all around, soaking the clothes of the people who were nearest, dotting their faces. A man wiped a finger over his face then licked away the water.

"It is sweet!" he called out. "The water that was bitter is now clean and delicious."

A great roar went up, one that in just seconds transformed itself into a song of praise for the Hebrew God. All around Rana, women smiled and raised their eyes to the heavens. Men hurried away and came back with buckets to dip into the well.

A group of eager helpers moved forward, men and women who stationed themselves around the well, forming the people into a line and calling them forward when it was their turn. Women gave cups of water to the thirsty. Men directed those with waterskins to the side of the well and helped to fill each and every one.

"Our God is great!" a young woman nearby sang out. Her voice was so lilting, Rana couldn't help but look her way. The small amount of the hair that peeked from beneath the woman's headscarf was the color of the bear Rana had once seen exhibited in the marketplace. Brown with touches of madder as red as a sunset. Her eyes were a shade of brown like amber, and her skin was like nothing Rana had ever seen before. Smooth. Luminous. Rana looked down at her own hands, as dry and as cracked as the dirt at her feet. She touched a finger to her lips. They were as rough as sandstone, and Rana wondered how she and this young woman could be so very different. One of them looked as if she managed to weather the elements. The other—Rana's shoulders drooped—looked as if the elements had weathered her.

Sometime while Rana was thinking all this, the young woman drew nearer. "Once again," she cried out for all around them to hear, "we see that our God is great. He has shown us how much He loves us." The way the woman looked at Rana and smiled told her she expected a response.

"Great. Yes," Rana said, when all she really wanted to say was that she wished the line would move a little more quickly so that she could finally get a drink.

The young woman looked Rana up and down, and her eyes sparked with curiosity. She stepped even closer. "I do not know you. I am Keziah, and it is always a pleasure to meet someone new. You must be camped with the brickmakers. That would explain why I have never seen you before. My brother will not let me go anywhere near the brickmakers. He says they are much too interested in the young women of the camp. If you are traveling with them, then you can tell me if it is true. My brother says the brickmakers want to find wives and I should stay out of their way. Only I do not know what is so terrible about a man finding me and making me his wife. Are you someone's wife? We are nearly the same age, I would guess, though I must say, you are much prettier than I am. But then, that hardly matters to a man, does it? They do not want wives they can look at and admire, they want good women who can give them sons and bake their bread. My brother, he says I am too young to marry, but I am all of eighteen years, much the same as you are yourself, I think."

If heat and thirst weren't enough to take Rana's breath away, the way Keziah talked as if her words were racing each other to escape her did. Even as they moved another few steps forward, Keziah kept on.

"What fun it will be to hear new things from a new person." As if sharing a secret, she leaned nearer, looked all around, and lowered her voice. "I see the same people. Day after day." She rolled her eyes. "There are only so many times you can hear the story of how their favorite child was born or how they once escaped a crocodile at the Nile. Yes, yes, I know." She held up a hand as if she expected Rana to speak, though the way Keziah went on and on, Rana was sure she wouldn't be able to say anything even if she wanted to. "It does sound like it would be a thrilling story, doesn't it? The crocodile, I mean. I suppose it was thrilling the first time I heard it." She sighed. "But after the second time and the third time and the fourth time…" Keziah threw back her head and laughed. "There, I have told you about me, and my name. And you are—"

"Very thirsty." Rana looked ahead to gauge their place in line. "It is a shame we cannot move to the well any faster."

"It is, isn't it?" Her nose wrinkling, Keziah thought about this. But only for a moment. The next second, she was off. "The more hands there are to help, the sooner everyone can get water," she called back to Rana. "I will offer my assistance."

Just as quickly as she'd appeared, she was off again, and Rana was left feeling breathless. Keziah was like the *Khamsin* she'd heard told of in stories, the mighty wind that blows across the desert and upends everything in its path. Once she was gone—already there at the front of the crowd handing out cups of water to the oldest people—Rana was able to sink back into solitude.

She could not help herself. While she stood there waiting, she looked around the crowd, half expecting to find Asim the Medjay looking back at her. When she didn't, she breathed a sigh of relief, moved forward a few more steps, and had another thought. This one much more interesting

The Hebrews around her were chatting and laughing, praising their God and calling out to each other. They had seen something wondrous happen—the bitter water had become sweet. And, unlike Rana, who wondered what kind of magic the man who threw the tree into the water must have and how he had called it down without the assistance of a temple or a sacrifice, they were celebrating, distracted.

And as she had learned in her years of hunting in the marketplace, distracted people are often careless. Unfortunately, a quick look at those around her told Rana these people were plain and simple. They had nothing worth stealing. That is, until a flash of carnelian caught her eye.

Keeping an eye on the wink of color, she slipped between the two men in front of her and sidled around a man and woman with their arms linked. She couldn't say she expected it, but it was just as she hoped. Chava, the woman with the beautiful bracelet. She was standing in the line for water, not two yards away.

The line moved forward, and Rana went along with it. It would be Chava's turn soon, and once she was busy, once she was distracted, Rana would have the perfect chance to make a move.

Chava stepped to the front of the line.

Rana moved in close behind her. The clasp of the bracelet was near enough to touch. She put out a hand, flicked the golden latch with thumb and forefinger, watched the bracelet loosen on Chava's wrist, and—

When someone stepped on Rana's foot, it was only natural she would think of her days in Pithom and about the way another thief who already had an eye on the bracelet would do anything to make sure Rana didn't get to it first.

Just as she would have done then, she knew that now, she had to fight.

She spun, her fists raised to defend herself, and her prize. And found herself looking at Keziah.

"I am so sorry!" Keziah put a hand on Rana's shoulder. "I did not mean to... I was so busy..." As if to prove it, she held up a cup of water. "I did not see you standing there, and I never meant to trample you. And you, my newest friend! You must think I am very rude."

"I think..." Rana lowered her hands and unclenched her fists. There would be no fight over the bracelet or anything else. Chava had her drink; she was already gone. Heat climbed into Rana's cheeks, and she turned toward the well. "Water," she said. "I think I would like a drink of water."

"Of course." Keziah filled a cup and offered it to Rana. "I can be clumsy at times. I do not always stop to think about what I am doing. At least that is what my brother tells me." The smile she gave Rana wobbled around the edges. "You do forgive me, do you not?"

It might have been the water wedged in Rana's throat that made it impossible for her to respond. Or it might have been that she turned and raced away from the well so quickly, she didn't have time to say anything to Keziah.

She knew only that when she finally pushed her way out of the crowd, she couldn't keep a question from whirling through her mind.

What kind of magic did the Hebrews have?

First a man changed bitter water to sweet.

And now, something had happened that had never happened to her before in her life. Someone had apologized to her. Apologized, and meant it.

What kind of people were these Hebrews that they could truly be nice to one another?

CHAPTER SEVEN

The question tickled at Rana's mind. So much so that the next day when they were told to fill their waterskins one more time before starting again into the wilderness, she found herself dwelling on it. She fell in with a group of women and, still searching for the answer to the puzzle that perplexed her, decided to observe them as they walked. She listened in on their conversations, noticed who their friends were, who they walked with, who they avoided. All the while she wondered, could these people who had so recently been slaves and were now traveling in the harshest conditions still be kind to each other?

What she discovered were small acts of thoughtfulness and signs of friendship she'd never before taken the time to notice.

An old woman had trouble walking, and two girls who could not have been old enough to see even twelve Akhets, the annual season of inundation along the Nile, propped her between them and helped her along.

A small child whined and fussed and refused to quiet down no matter how hard his harried mother tried to still him, and a woman with a gentle smile scooped the child out of his mother's arms and held him close and cooed a song.

A young girl stumbled, scraped her knee, and cried, and her friends gathered around her and told her amusing stories until her tears dried and she smiled once again.

It seemed that, to the Hebrews, nothing about any of this behavior was out of the ordinary. Yet seeing it left Rana stunned and shaken. It was a new way of looking at the world, one that felt as unfamiliar as if she'd woken up and found herself living in the clouds, and she worked her way through it just as she would if she were walking on clouds, one careful step at a time.

"You will take a meal with us, of course," one of the women said to Rana. They had stopped to rest when the sun was at its highest and the air was as hot against their skin as the heat of an oven. The woman patted the rock next to her by way of inviting Rana to sit. "We have bread left from last evening. It is not the freshest, but—"

"I would be..." It took Rana a moment to find the word. "I would be grateful," she said, and she realized she meant it.

They rested there for the afternoon and started out again when the sun slipped lower and the sky was touched with orange and red and the pink of a flamingo, the embodiment of the sun god, Ra.

Yet, these Hebrews did not believe in Ra, or in any of the other gods Rana had always known to rule the sky above, the earth below, and the underworld. The Israelites believed in just one God, the proof of His existence being the pillar that guided their travels and lit the nighttime, the way He'd delivered them from Egypt, the fact that the water in Marah had gone from bitter to sweet at the bidding of His servant.

And that made Rana think and wonder all the more.

Even those thoughts, though, flew from her head just as the last of the sun touched the sky and someone up ahead in the crowd cried out, "We are here! In Elim! Look, everyone. Look!"

Like the others all around her, Rana raced forward. They were on top of a rise and looking down at the vast plain below—

Rana's breath escaped her in a gasp of pure wonder.

From where she stood on the hill, she could see twelve wells and dozens of palm trees, their branches laden with dates.

"Our God is wonderful!" a woman called out and raced past Rana and down to the wells. "Look at the paradise He has provided for us!"

It was a paradise, indeed, and Rana couldn't wait to rest in the shade of a palm tree. The people surged forward and, like them, Rana made a move toward the path to the oasis, eager to bite into a sweet date and feel the blessings of cool water on her forehead.

Yet she stopped just as she was about to step on the path. An old couple, their arms linked, stepped forward, and Rana let them start down ahead of her.

That night, Rana slept better than she had since they started out from Pithom, and she woke refreshed. It helped that she had poured water over her head before she lay down in a soft patch of sand beneath a sprawling palm. On rising, she ate dates and drank at one of the cool, fresh wells, and after, because they had been told they'd be staying there for several days, she walked the camp to get better acquainted with its layout.

Not an easy thing with a camp that stretched as far as she could see, east and west, north and south. And with so many people! It was no wonder the lords of Egypt were reluctant to let the Hebrew slaves leave. There were tens of thousands of them, and the work of their hands surely helped the land of Egypt reach greatness. Not to mention make its bricks, rear its children, tend its gardens.

She wondered what was happening in Egypt now, how her people were coping without legions of slaves to do their work, but she set the thought aside. She would find out soon enough, she promised herself, as soon as she found a way to return to her country.

She was so busy thinking about all this, she didn't realize how far she'd wandered until she found herself at the perimeter of the camp and saw a large number of men gathered there. They were soldiers, the ones commanded by the man named Joshua whom she'd heard spoken of with respect. Some had swords drawn and they were drilling, fighter against fighter, their expressions fixed and serious. The crack of metal on metal echoed against the distant hills. Across a wide expanse of open land, others practiced their archery skills, and not far away, a few dozen men wrestled, grunts and groans punctuating their every move. The men closest to where Rana stood lifted large bags filled with sand with just one hand, their faces red, their cheeks puffed from the effort. Except for one, that is. His back to her, he lifted a heavy bag and held it high above his head, long enough that his comrades finally applauded his effort, and when he dropped the bag and it thudded to the ground, they clapped him on the back to congratulate him.

An impressive display of strength, and Rana might have continued to watch. That is, until the man turned to get a drink of water and she saw it was Gideon.

Their gazes met, but only for a heartbeat. Rana whirled around and hurried away.

To be sure she did not run into him again, she did not return to the camp the way she came but roamed a little farther still. After days of traveling with thousands of people, the hubbub of the camp, the braying of donkeys and the bleating of sheep, the quiet of the wilderness was a change, and Rana was surprised how much she reveled in it.

She breathed deep, drinking in a silence interrupted only by a sound she couldn't identify. It was soft and secret, like fingers sliding over linen, and Rana slowed her breathing to keep tempo with it. She shut her eyes, enjoying the play of colors the dazzling sun created against her lids. Except for that soft swish and the far-off call of birds, it was peaceful there in Elim, and though she wasn't sure she'd ever considered it before, she realized now what a luxury that was. Peace. Quiet. Plenty of water. It was confusing, then, to think she'd heard the Hebrews say this wasn't their ultimate destination. They planned to venture farther still into the wilderness.

Of course that didn't mean she had to go with them.

The idea came out of nowhere, and it filled Rana with a jolt like lightning. Her shoulders shot back. She smiled. Elim was an oasis of great beauty. Many travelers must stop there. When the Hebrews left, there was nothing to say she couldn't stay behind. Sooner or later, a caravan was bound to come by, and with any luck, it would be headed to Egypt.

Excitement tapped at Rana's insides, and when she started back to the camp, her steps were light, and that same, repeated soft sound—one she still heard but whose source she could not discover—was in perfect tempo to her breaths.

She congratulated herself. Finally, she had found a solution to her problem and a way back to Egypt.

Though she was cheerful enough to hum a tune, she was sure the song that drifted to her ears did not come from her own lips. The voice was pleasant, and as airy as a wealthy woman's veil. Light. Lovely.

Except that, as far as Rana could see—she looked all around—there was no one anywhere near who could be singing.

Had the sun finally gotten the best of her and addled her brain? When she made her way around a boulder higher than two men, she saw she had nothing to worry about.

Keziah, the girl who had stomped on her foot near the well at Marah, stood not far away, looking out over the expanse of plains around them, the mountains on the far horizon, the dome of blue sky above their heads. She was singing softly to herself.

Keziah was clearly lost in her thoughts. She had no idea Rana was nearby, and a lifetime of experience told Rana it was best to keep it that way. She was skilled at staying in the background and not calling attention to herself. Her life had always depended on it. Yet she thought of how Keziah had offered her an unexpected apology, and before she could stop herself, she called out, "What are you doing over there?"

Keziah turned, smiled, and waved. "Nothing really," she yelled back, kicking at the rocky ground. "Just walking and relaxing. The shepherds have been this way. See?" She pointed to a nearby low-growing shrub, and to see what she was talking about and what it had to do with shepherds, Rana stepped closer. Just as she had been the last time she saw Keziah, she was again struck by the smoothness of her skin, the touch of color in her cheeks.

"Look!" Keziah ran a hand over the branches of the shrub to show that here and there, it was dotted with wool. "It looks as if the wool grows right on the plant, doesn't it?"

"There is no such plant as that." Rana was sure of it.

Keziah laughed. "No. There isn't. When the shepherds brought their flocks this way, the coats of the sheep got tangled in the branches of the shrubs. The wool was tugged off and left behind. The spinners know this happens all the time, so they follow along after the shepherds. They will come this way later, and they will pick the wool from the plants. For now"—she breathed in deep and let the breath out in a long, contented sigh that reminded Rana of the soft sound she'd heard earlier—"I am pretending there is such a plant. One that sprouts wool as soft as a baby's cheek and as light as feathers. I am imagining that we will see it and other such wonderous things when we finally arrive in Canaan."

All through their journey, Rana had heard the Hebrews talk of a place called Canaan, but she knew if she asked what she really wanted to know—where it was and why it was so important for the Hebrews to go there—Keziah would uncover the truth about her and realize she did not belong, so instead she said, "Is it far to Canaan?"

Keziah shrugged. "I have no head for such things. Distances. And days. And how we know where, exactly, we're going or how we are going to get there. That is why we have wise leaders like Moses and Aaron. And I have my brother, of course, to explain things to me when I do not understand, though I must say, he is not always as patient as I wish he would be."

The very idea soured Rana's mouth. "This brother, he is cruel to you?"

"Oh, no. Not at all." Keziah put a hand on Rana's arm by way of thanking her for her concern. "He is as kind as any brother can be. It is just that sometimes he is… Well, I suppose he is preoccupied. He has other things to think about. Other duties to attend to. You know, like all men do. That means when I ask my silly questions… How far do we walk in any one day? How do we know we are headed in the right direction? What does Canaan look like, and how will we know when we finally arrive there? When I ask questions such as that, he sometimes does not have the time to explain things to me, and I am left as confused as I was before I ever asked."

"And your mother and father? What do they say when you ask them?"

Keziah looked away. "My abba was one of the men charged with raising a statue in a new temple built for the pleasure of Pharaoh. It was a very large statue, and heavy. The ropes broke. My abba was crushed beneath the image of a heathen god. My imma…" She cleared her throat. "She missed him terribly. One day she simply fell asleep and never woke up again. I believe she could not bear the thought of living without the man she loved." She gave Rana a sidelong look.

"I asked you when we first met, but you never told me. Do you have a husband? Or at least a man you love?" she asked Rana.

"I do not."

"Is there one you have your eye on? Some man you met back in Egypt or someone your family has always said would be a good match for you? Or maybe there is someone you have seen here in the camp and he has caught your eye? A man you know is from a good family who is a hard worker and will provide for you?"

When Rana didn't answer, Keziah poked her in the ribs with her elbow. "You know exactly what I am talking about. That one man you think has not noticed you yet, but you would really like him to."

It wasn't that she'd never thought about it, it was just that Rana knew a woman like her did not find a man, settle down, start a family. "Not that I have ever found," she said.

"But you would like one, of course. A husband, I mean."

Rana pursed her lips and confessed, "I sometimes like the idea of it."

Keziah laughed. "The idea of it! You make it sound like some dream that will never come true, and we both know it is bound to happen sooner or later for all of us women. A woman needs a man to take care of her. A man needs a woman so he can have a family. How lucky I will be when I have a husband." She gave Rana a careful look. "Isn't that how you feel? How nice it would be if we were traveling with our husbands and their families."

Rana knew the truth. It was hard to steal enough to feed one mouth. To provide for two would be nearly impossible. "And if I did"—she smiled at Keziah to let her know she was teasing—"it would be unfitting for you to ask like you did, if I had my eye on someone."

Keziah stifled a laugh. "My brother says it is inappropriate of me to ask personal questions of people. But how will I really get to know you if I do not know what you are thinking? He says I should not so openly discuss things like love and marriage either. But then, he has not seen the things I have seen." She gave Rana a wink.

"And what does that mean?" Rana couldn't wait to hear more.

"Just that I was a house slave to a wealthy and beautiful woman," Keziah explained, warming to the subject, her eyes twinkling. "She had no husband, so she did not have to worry about being faithful to anyone. She had many suitors. Some of them were very handsome. And they were all men of wealth and status. Oh, how they ached for her! They courted her with jewels and food and exotic animals, and she gave them wine, and they spent nights together in the moonlight, dancing and frolicking. That is not the kind of husband I want," she added, as if it were actually in the realm of possibility. "I do not need jewels. I want nothing more than a good man. A kind man. One who works hard and cares for me and—"

"Hush!" Rana held out a hand to stop Keziah. Again, she'd heard the faint sound. Confounded by it and the way it seemed to follow her, she was determined to find its source. "Listen."

Keziah bent her head. "Listen to what?" she wanted to know. "I hear nothing."

"Nor do I. Not now. But earlier and again now, I thought I heard…" Rana strained her ears. "Some sound. Like the swishing of an ostrich-feather fan."

"I think you need to get back to the clamor of the camp. The quiet and the wind are playing tricks on your ears," Keziah insisted.

But Rana wasn't so sure. She listened for a few more moments and, hearing nothing, turned to walk away.

And that is when she saw it. There, among the rocks not far from where Keziah stood.

It had the perfect camouflage, the same reddish-brown color as the rocky ground. And the swishing sound? Yes, Rana had heard the stories, and she should have remembered. It moved side to side, sliding over the sand and stony ground. Quick and quiet. Deadly.

"Do not move," she commanded Keziah in a rough whisper. "There is a horned viper not far from you."

Keziah's face paled. Her body stiffened. "You are wrong, surely," she insisted, but Rana could tell by her eyes—suddenly large and round—she knew Rana was telling the truth.

"The snake has two horns," Rana said. "One over each eye. It is very near your left foot. No—" She put out a hand when Keziah made the instinctive move to dash away. "They are very quick."

"And very deadly." A single tear slipped down Keziah's cheek. "What can we do?"

The truth of the matter was that Rana didn't know. But she could hardly tell Keziah that. The smart thing to do was for her to turn and run, to leave Keziah to her fate, to not risk herself, to not put her life in danger. She had lived her entire life by those rules. But one look at Keziah's shaking hands, the way her knees gave way, and Rana knew the smartest thing was not right.

She swallowed hard. "You must keep as still as the stones themselves," she told Keziah. "I will get…" She looked at the ground and spied a rock small enough to hold, thick enough to inflict damage. "I am going to have to move very quickly, but you must not—"

"Can you move quickly enough? So quickly the creature will not know—"

"I have had some experience moving fast enough to keep from being noticed," Rana said, and she wondered if Keziah could imagine it was a confession of sorts. Without ever taking her eyes off the snake, she bent her knees, reached out to her left, and grabbed the rock. She hefted it in her hand.

Keziah ran her tongue over her lips. "What if when you throw the rock, you hit me instead of the snake?"

"I have no intention of throwing the rock," Rana assured her, and then, before she could tell herself she was being foolhardy at best, she leaped forward. She brought the rock down on the snake's head before it had a chance to move.

Keziah wailed her relief, and her knees gave way. "Thank you, thank you." She made to grab Rana's hand but changed her mind when she realized Rana still held the rock, smeared now with the blood of the snake. She shot to her feet and stepped away.

"It is all right. You are fine now." Because Keziah's gaze was still on the rock, Rana tossed it aside. She rubbed her palms against her woolen tunic and lied to calm Keziah. "You were never really in any danger."

"If I was never really in any danger..." Keziah looked at the smashed remains of the snake. "You would not have dispatched the creature if it was not a threat. And if I had stayed out here on my own, if you had not walked by and seen me, if you had not come over and talked to me—" With a sound that was half cry, half laugh, she threw herself at Rana and wrapped her in a hug. "You saved my life. Thank you. You are..." Keziah backed away, the better to look

Rana up and down. "You are very brave. And very fast. My goodness, how does a woman learn to move so quickly and so quietly?"

The half smile Rana gave her in return was meant as an answer, but Keziah would have none of it.

"You must explain it to me. You must tell me everything about yourself. After all, you saved my life, and that means that we are great friends now." She reached for Rana's hand, and when she did, Keziah wrinkled her nose. "Your skin is as rough as the abrasive sand the stonecutters use to smooth their works. What have you been doing to it?"

Rana's laugh was one of amazement rather than amusement. "Walking in the glaring sun. Sleeping in the wilderness. Killing serpents with my bare hands."

"Yes, yes. Of course." Keziah looped an arm through hers and led her back to the camp. "I have something I think will help."

CHAPTER EIGHT

Keziah's tent was larger than that of Leah, the spinner Rana had broken bread with. There were rushes scattered over the ground, a rug on top of them, baskets along two of the cloth walls, and an opening high above a small burning pit at the very center of the tent. A fire inside on cold nights. What a luxury it must be!

It was too hot that day to think about a fire inside, but outside the doorway, Rana had seen small, sputtering flames, and grain waiting to be milled. Since she had never thought much about a life of domesticity, she did not know for certain, but it seemed to her that if Keziah intended to become someone's wife, she would need to concentrate more on her household duties and less on wandering in the vast emptiness that surrounded them, singing.

The thought warmed Rana's heart, and she shifted uncomfortably, as if changing her stance and the set of her shoulders would help her better understand the unfamiliar emotion. She had never had a friend before, not one outside the circle of thieves back in Pithom who cared less about her and more about whether she would give them a portion of what she'd stolen that day or a sip of the beer she'd bought with her takings. Keziah's constant chattering was dizzying, that was certain, but it made Rana smile.

And like friends, smiles had been in short supply back in Egypt.

Her own did not last long when she saw two cushions set at a low table inside the tent. Keziah had a brother. A brother who might not welcome an Egyptian intruder.

At the doorway, Rana held back. "I must be going," she told Keziah.

Keziah already had the lid of one large basket tossed aside and was rooting through it, and she looked at Rana in wonder. "Going where?"

Rana pointed in some indefinite direction over her shoulder. "I just need to—"

"Do not be silly." Keziah was at the doorway in an instant. She took Rana's hand, drew her farther into the tent, and urged her to sit on one of the cushions before she went back to the doorway and pinned back the flap to allow more air inside. "You saved my life."

"I was happy to do it," Rana told her, and it was the truth.

"You were not afraid of the horned viper."

"Oh, I was!" Another truth, and a shiver crawled up Rana's spine. "I have never been so close to a deadly creature. I was so afraid, my bones were rattling!"

Considering this, Keziah cocked her head. "And yet you did not run away. You stayed. You helped me."

Rana shrugged. "I do believe the idea of abandoning you and you being bitten and your body lying there in the wilderness..." She realized she'd spoken in a rush, so much like Keziah often did, and she took a deep breath before she laughed. "For some reason, that frightened me even more than the snake did."

Smiling, Keziah bustled back to the basket she'd been burrowing through and came to the table holding a wooden box. It was a pretty thing, no bigger than the span of three hands, and beautifully decorated with inlaid wood and inscriptions Rana could not read. "You were frightened, but still you helped me. Then you can fully understand why I need to show my appreciation." She set the box on the table and plopped onto the second cushion. "Go ahead." She waved toward Rana. "Set your hands here on the table."

Rana looked at the box. She looked at Keziah. "Why?"

"You are brave enough to kill a deadly viper with nothing but a rock, yet you are afraid of what I might do to your hands?" Keziah dissolved into a fit of giggles. When she finished laughing, she motioned toward the table again. "Trust me."

Trust was another unfamiliar emotion. It fluttered through Rana like butterfly wings, tickling her insides. It was a strange feeling, but much to Rana's surprise, it was not unpleasant.

She set her hands on the table. "What are you going to do to me?" Her voice faltered, and she scolded herself. Once for her cowardice. Another time because she let it show. "Will it hurt?"

"Actually, it might sting a bit. But—" When Rana flinched and made to pull her hands away, Keziah rolled her eyes. "The prickling will only be for a moment. I promise. And besides…" She unlatched the lid on the wooden box. "It is a good sort of stinging, and when it is over, you will feel glorious. Or at least your hands will."

Rana wasn't so sure there was such a thing as good stinging, but now that Keziah had the box opened, she didn't budge. She was too interested to see what was inside.

The top of the box was hinged, and when Keziah lifted it, Rana saw that nestled beneath the lid was a copper hand mirror that shone like the sun, even in the dim light inside the tent. The mirror was shaped like the sun too. Round, except at the bottom where it was slightly flattened, and Rana knew that like all such small mirrors, it was fashioned to represent the sun on the horizon. The handle of the mirror looked to be made of copper too, but she couldn't be certain; it was wrapped with linen. Keziah took the mirror from the box and unwound the fabric, and Rana looked at the figure wrought there in metal, a beautiful icon, a woman wearing a headdress of cow horns with the sun disc between them.

Keziah bent her head closer to Rana and whispered, "See. The handle is an idol, made in the image of an Egyptian goddess."

Rana nodded. "Hathor. She is the goddess of beauty."

"Fitting for a mirror, don't you think?" Keziah asked. "But my brother would not be happy if he saw it, would he?"

No, Rana imagined he would not be. Hathor was the mother of Horus, god of the sky, and Ra, the sun god. As such, she was the mother of all pharaohs. These were the gods of the Egyptian people, not the Hebrews.

"Hebrews worship one God, not many as the Egyptians do," Rana said, thinking out loud, considering all it meant in relation to the way she had always believed the world worked. "To you, the figure is not sacred or magical as it might be to an Egyptian. The figure there on the mirror, to you, it is nothing more than adornment?"

Keziah grinned. "You make it sound like a question. As if you do not understand the difference between our beliefs and those of the Egyptians. But..." She gave Rana a wink. "Adornment. I will remember that if my brother ever catches sight of the mirror. I will remind him I know full well the figure has no power, no magic. It is just adornment. And I will promise him what I have promised myself. When I have the chance, I will remove Hathor and discard the handle in the desert where no one will ever find her. I will replace the handle with a plain piece of wood."

"Yet the copper handle…" Rana studied it. "It is valuable, surely, and something that precious—"

"It is not as important as being true to our God, is it?" When Keziah set the mirror on the table, she covered it again with the cloth. "I would never want anyone to think I did not honor the One True God. No, Hathor will have to go! But for now…"

Again, Keziah reached for the box. There was a drawer at the front of it, and she slid it open. Inside was a wooden panel fashioned to fit the drawer perfectly. There were eight holes in the panel, a small ointment jar nestled in each hole. She plucked out one jar and set it on the table.

The jar was made of stone the color of a pigeon's bosom, perfectly round at the top, but tapered toward the bottom, the better to fit into its proper compartment so that when the box was moved, the jars did not clatter against each other. Keziah removed the lid of the jar to reveal a white cream, and the scent of almonds and honey tickled Rana's nose. She breathed deep and smiled.

She had smelled such glorious aromas only once before, when she caught a temple priest unaware and made off with the linen handkerchief he'd made the mistake of setting down at a market stall. How many times had she held it close, breathing in the wonderful scents that had perfumed the priest and soaked into the cloth? How sad it was when, after many months, the odors of the streets of Pithom—of desperation and hunger—masked the pleasing smell and the cloth lost its charm.

Rana leaned closer for a better look at the cream in the ointment jar. "What is it?"

"Skin cream, of course." Keziah dipped two fingers into the pot, plopped the cream on them onto Rana's right hand, and rubbed it into her skin.

She was right. It did sting. Rana winced.

"It only prickles because your skin is so dry," Keziah said. "I will put some cream on your left hand too." She did. "And once it has all had a chance to soak in, we will apply a little more. By that time, it will not hurt at all."

As Keziah had promised, it was a good kind of hurt. Uncomfortable at first. Then refreshing. Then, as foolish as it seemed, Rana could have sworn the cream was nourishing her skin. And it smelled…

Rana put her hands to her nose so she could breathe deep. "It smells delicious."

"Well, you are not going to eat any of it." Keziah laughed. "But yes, it does smell good, doesn't it? Here, closer." With one hand, she waved Rana nearer and put some of the cream on her cheeks. "The hot sun has done little good to any of our skin, and I must say, yours is worse than most. It is like you have lived outside all your life. Let the cream absorb on your face for a few minutes."

While Rana did as she was instructed, a realization hit. "This is why your skin is so smooth and beautiful," she told Keziah. "You have had the benefit of this wonderful cream. Tell me, are the other women here in the camp jealous?"

As if it was nothing at all, Keziah waved away the question. "I would be happy to share if they asked."

Rana looked over the other ointment jars still nestled in the box. "And what other wonders do you have to share?"

One by one, Keziah pulled out the jars. One contained red cream. "Rouge," Keziah said, "for lips and cheeks." She rubbed a bit onto Rana's cheeks and spread a little more on her lips. "And this one..." She lifted the lid of another jar. "This is henna powder, used to color the fingernails. We do not have time to use that on your nails now, but we will try it another time. And this, this is my favorite." She whisked off another lid. "This is kohl."

"To outline the eyes," Rana said.

"And a good Hebrew woman..." Keziah laughed. "She would never use such powders and paints. They are reserved for Egyptians."

"Which makes me wonder, Keziah, how you obtained such prizes."

Even without the benefits of the contents of the rouge pot, Keziah's cheeks flushed a sunset color.

It was an interesting enough response to make Rana curious. "You said you were a slave to a wealthy woman, and I am sure wealthy women have all these wonders and more. Keziah, did you steal these things?"

Keziah groaned and crumpled. "Now that you know I am dishonest, you will think less of me."

If she didn't have her head on the table, she would have seen Rana smile. "Truth be told, I admire your backbone."

Keziah sat up. "Do you really?" She made a face. "But that does not make what I did right, does it?"

Rana had spent little time thinking of right and wrong. Practical. Convenient. Necessary. These things seemed far more useful to a life on the streets than thoughts of honesty or ethics. If the Hebrews based their actions on such concepts, she had a great deal to learn, both about the people and their beliefs. Until then, it seemed more important to relieve Keziah's worries. "You knew your days as a slave were over?" she asked her friend.

Keziah nodded.

"And you knew you were leaving Egypt and never going back?"

Again, Keziah agreed.

"So you decided—"

"That my mistress, she had this beautiful box and this lovely mirror, and pots and pots of oils and perfumes and cosmetics. What would a little of this and a little of that mean to her? I am sure she has not missed any of it yet. That she never will. Still..." Her eyes welled. "It was a terrible thing to do, wasn't it?"

The answer seemed simple enough. At least to Rana. "Without you doing what you think is a terrible thing, my hands would not feel nearly this good."

Keziah sniffled. "Yes, that bit of good has come out of it."

"And without you being able to make my hands feel so good, you could not have paid me back for saving your life today."

Keziah's shoulders shot back. "That is true. And I am so glad the cream is working its magic. My mistress, she had so much. These little jars were meant just for when she traveled."

"And now you are the one traveling."

"I am."

"And helping a friend whose skin is the worst you have ever seen."

"It really is. You must come visit me every day so that you can apply more cream to your hands and face."

"And use up all you have? No, that would not be right."

Keziah shrugged off her concerns. "There was a woman in my mistress's household, her name was Anippe. She knew the best ways to produce cosmetics, and she shared her knowledge with me. The ingredients, they are not so easy to come by here in the camp, but once we get to Canaan, I know I will find everything I need. Canaan is going to be a paradise! And when we are finally there, I will make pots and pots of creams, and the women, they will flock to me. Until then, you and I, we will treat ourselves to what I have. You must also visit the spinners. They will share the lanolin they clean from the wool, and lanolin is very good for your skin. You never knew spinners who offered you lanolin? Not even back in Goshen?"

Rana sidestepped the question. "I have met a spinner here in the camp. A woman called Leah."

"My family knows Leah. She is a good woman. I searched for her soon after we started out from Pithom, but you know what chaos it was. I would be happy to see her again. You must take me to her tent."

Rana did not agree, and Keziah didn't notice. She was too busy preparing the kohl powder and taking out one of the thin ivory sticks Rana knew was used to apply it. "Here. Come closer. I will outline your eyes the way the wealthy women do. You will have to wash your face before you go back outside into the camp, but for now, wouldn't you like to see yourself as a beautiful Egyptian woman?"

It was too good an offer, and Rana wished she did not have to wash the kohl away. Aside from enhancing the look of the eyes, she knew kohl helped deflect the glare of the sun.

A few moments later, Keziah sat back and smiled, pleased with her handiwork. "You look like a priestess!"

Not a compliment Rana had ever thought to get. She motioned to Keziah for the mirror and looked into it, and her mouth fell open.

A fine Egyptian lady looked back at her.

Well, except for the scarf that covered her head.

Rana whisked it away. Her hair was the color of *kem*, the life-giving silt left by the Nile's annual flooding, and she smoothed it over her shoulders.

She'd had glimpses of her face before. Reflected in water. Blinking back at her from a glass amulet. But she had never had a chance to really study it, to compare it to those of the women she saw at the market or processing to the temples, to the Hebrews she had met there in the camp. Though her eyes were hollowed by the constant hunger that gnawed at her belly and her skin was still rough in those places Keziah's cream had not touched, she was not so different from them. In fact, she had to admit, her face was far more pleasing than most. Her features were even. Her nose was not too large or too pointed. The kohl Keziah had applied so expertly around her eyes made her look older, and she would have said regal if not for the fact that the very idea of a street girl looking noble and sophisticated made her chuckle.

Keziah wrinkled her nose. "You are laughing. You do not like looking like an Egyptian."

"I do. I think it is the most wonderful thing I have ever seen. Truly." She reached across the table and squeezed Keziah's hand. "I was just thinking how odd it is, that is all. How I look like myself, and yet like someone else."

Keziah pursed her lips. "Maybe that someone else, maybe I would know her name?"

Rana pulled her hand back to her lap. "You think me rude."

"I think you think I am not so good a friend as I think you are."

It took Rana a moment to consider this statement. It was no use, it made no sense from any angle. "You think you are a better friend than I am? Because—"

"You will not reveal your name."

When Keziah looked at her that way, pouting and with her large, dark eyes wide and wounded, Rana decided she knew for the very first time what guilt must feel like. Her heart squeezed, and regret fluttered through her then took root, like a rock in her stomach.

"I am sorry," Rana said. "I did not mean to insult you. I thought only to—"

Only thought to what? Protect herself? Hide herself? Keep to that solitary and lonely place she'd always thought was her life?

She swallowed around the sudden tightness in her throat. "I am Rana."

Keziah's sudden grin was as bright as the sun. "And I am very happy to be your friend, Rana. I think we will be like sisters, don't you?"

Rana coughed away the tremor in her voice that threatened to betray the sudden rush of gratitude that coursed through her. The sudden, unexpected satisfaction of putting down roots, even ones so small and tenuous. "I would like that," she said.

"Except, you do not already have a sister, do you? For I would hate to have your sister get angry with me for stealing away your friendship. Tell me. Tell me all about your family."

Searching for the words that would satisfy Keziah, Rana ran her tongue over her lips. She was about to spout a lie about a father who was long dead and a mother who had stayed behind in Egypt to care for an elderly uncle, when a shadow darkened the door and a man strode into the tent.

Keziah rose to greet him.

"Come here. You must meet my new friend." She wound an arm through his and pulled him closer. "This is my new friend, Rana. And Rana, I am so happy you are here now so that you two can meet. This is my brother, Gideon."

CHAPTER NINE

If he was surprised to see Rana there in his tent, Gideon didn't show it. His face a mask, each of his movements methodical and precise, he unfastened the scabbard that held his sword at his side and carefully set the weapon atop the nearest basket. He slipped the bow from his left shoulder and set that down too, along with the quiver that held his arrows. He was a careful man, and completely controlled, and Rana thought that was unfortunate. She would have preferred to see some sign of what he was thinking. A flare of shock. A look of suspicion. Even a flash of anger. Then she would know if his emotions were suddenly as upside down as hers.

Were his insides fidgety? Because her stomach was suddenly swooping like a kestrel. She flattened her hands against the table as if it might serve to anchor her, but still, her stomach bunched. Her heart skipped a beat right before it sped up like one of the racing horses she saw during festivals, their bareback riders as fearless as she, suddenly, was not. It was one thing confronting a man like Gideon in the open air. It was another altogether meeting him face to face. In private. In his own home.

She swallowed hard, grateful that Gideon had gone to where a bowl of water was set out and was busy splashing water on his face, dashing it over his muscular arms, scrubbing it over the back of his neck. He was too busy to pay any notice of her, and while he was, she flicked the linen cloth over the Hathor mirror and shot Keziah a quick look. The secret was theirs to keep.

When Gideon was done, Keziah handed him a cloth to dry himself. It wasn't until he was finished and gave the cloth back to Keziah that he turned toward their guest. Like the first time she'd seen him, the corners of his mouth dipped into a scowl. Like the last time they'd encountered each other when he spoiled her attempt to make off with Chava's beautiful bracelet, his gaze was steady and unwavering. There was no warmth in his eyes.

"Rana—it is an Egyptian name," he said.

Keziah was a girl who sang in the wilderness. Even if she heard the challenge ring through Gideon's voice, she would not understand what it meant. Not like Rana did. Keziah didn't feel the spark of her brother's gaze. Not as strongly as Rana felt it. She did not notice, as Rana did, that his spine was as straight as one of his arrows, that his hands curled into fists at his sides. If she did, Keziah would not have laughed.

"Of course Rana is an Egyptian name." With the cloth he'd used to dry himself, she gave his arm a playful slap. "We have all just come from Egypt, have we not? Our people have lived there for more than four hundred years. Is it so odd, then, that one of us would have an Egyptian name?"

"One of…us?" Gideon's gaze raked Rana. The kohl painted near her eyes. The rouge that colored her cheeks. "Yes, I do believe that would be odd."

"Well, odd or not, that is her name. And she is my new friend. I have asked her here today because—"

"Because..." When Gideon's gaze swung from her to the fine wooden box, Rana let go of the breath she'd been holding. "You insist on wasting your time with trivial things, Sister, when you should be attending to your household chores."

Keziah's expression fell. It was not so much that she was angry at her brother. Or that she chafed under his criticism. She was disappointed. Rana could tell from the way her shoulders slumped and her fingers twisted around the cloth, bunching it into her palm. Keziah expected more from Gideon. More understanding, and perhaps a little kindness. She expected her brother to be delighted that she'd found a friend. And he had fallen short on all counts.

"I was not wasting time." As if it might actually help him see reason, she stomped one foot. "I invited Rana here because—"

"Have you checked to see if all our pottery is still where it should be? If our oil lamps are where you last left them?" He looked all around. "You can never be too careful, you know. Sometimes things disappear. Donkeys, for instance."

He would have to do better than that if he meant to wound Rana with his words, and realizing it, a wave of courage flooded her. After all, the donkey was back where it belonged, and Chava's bracelet hadn't been in her possession for more than a minute or two.

"It is a good thing we are simple people with no fine jewelry," Gideon added, as if he knew exactly what she was thinking. "We would need to be careful with that too. Especially when there is"—his gaze swung to Rana—"a stranger in our home."

"A stranger who will trouble you no longer." Rana rose from her seat. "Perhaps I will see you again in the camp," she told Keziah before she looked toward Gideon. "Or perhaps I will not. I think your brother, he does not approve of our friendship, or of me."

"Then he is a fool." It was as simple as that. At least to Keziah. She stepped back, tilted her head, and squinted her eyes to give her brother a careful look. "If you would let me explain, Gideon, you will realize you are acting no better than one of the donkeys out in the pens."

Rana couldn't help but smile.

Gideon's gaze swung to Rana. "Is it funny to hear a sister admonish a brother so?" he wanted to know.

She was grateful she'd had time to collect herself so she could respond, "Yes, it is quite funny. Especially since it is true."

He threw his hands in the air and slapped them against his sides. "Both of you? You sat here with your heads together and decided you would lie in wait for me, then both be insolent?"

"We did not need to decide," Rana told him. "Some things just come naturally. Besides, you no longer have to deal with two of us, only one." She slipped past Keziah and her brother and moved toward the doorway. "I have no wish to upset your household or to cause trouble."

"Oh, no!" Keziah grabbed her arm. She was a small, wiry girl with a surprisingly strong grip. "You are not leaving. Not until my brother hears what you did for me today. And you!" With her other hand, she latched onto Gideon, and before Rana knew it, Keziah had pivoted to stand to Rana's left and Gideon's right, and Rana was toe-to-toe with Gideon.

She'd forgotten how he towered over her. He, if the look in his eyes meant anything at all, had forgotten all those things he'd said that had warmed her heart.

Eyes like midnight on the Nile. Hair the color of the shadows. Now he looked at her as if he remembered none of it.

"You..." When Keziah squeezed her arm, Rana snapped out of her thoughts. "You will not leave, and you will not move one step more, not until I have had a chance to tell my brother what happened today. Do not let him scare you away. He can be a lout, but it is all an act. He is a soldier, you see, so he believes he must act strong and threatening even when he is not with his comrades. In truth, he is a good man, and soft-hearted and kind when he does not think he has something to prove."

She turned to her brother. "And you, you will stand right there. And you will listen. You will not interrupt. And you will stop being so rude. Did not Imma and Abba always teach us that we are to welcome strangers? Yet this is how you act? If you are angry at Rana about the Egyptian cosmetics, you should not be. They are mine, and I am the one who applied them to Rana's face, to show her how it is done and to thank her. Yes, to thank her. Because you see, Brother, if it were not for Rana, I would not be standing here talking to you right now."

He opened his mouth to speak. When he couldn't find the words, he snapped it shut again.

Keziah let go of him long enough to wag a finger. "Speak not a word. And know that I am not inventing stories. I have not been in the sun too long. I know what I am talking about. Hear me out. Yes, you are right. I was avoiding my household chores earlier today. I could not stand the thought of spending another moment grinding grain." She groaned. "Do you know how boring it is to grind for hours at a time? My muscles get sore. My brain gets weary. So I decided to rest, just for a while, and I walked not far from where you and the other soldiers were training. That is where Rana found me and joined me, and it was a good thing she did. There was a…" Her words caught on a sob, and she sniffed and swallowed hard. "There was a…" She sniffled again.

Rana couldn't bear to see her agonize over the memory. "There was a horned viper in the rocks," she told Gideon, her voice as even as the look she gave him. "Keziah might have been bitten."

"I would surely have been bitten," Keziah wailed. "I would have been, for the snake was very close. And I would be dead, Gideon, if Rana had not taken a rock and…" Remembering the scene, her face paled. "She took a rock, and she swung it with all her might, and she smashed the snake before it ever had a chance to move. She was so quick, and so fearless. She killed the viper. She saved my life."

There, the story was told, and because Keziah had already shown her such great kindness and she was sure she wouldn't get any thanks from Gideon, Rana knew it was time to go and leave brother and sister in peace. She pulled away from Keziah, whirled, and fled from the tent.

She was already well away from it, at a place where the sun made a pool of light between two standing stones, when she heard a voice call from behind her.

"Wait!"

It was Gideon, and she did not wait.

She refused to run from him. Instead, she marched just as she imagined he did when he was with his comrades, chin held high, arms close to her sides, putting as much distance from him as quickly as she could. In the time since the Hebrew God had made the waters of the Red Sea part and they'd started through the wilderness, Rana had been through every part of the camp. But it changed with each encampment; tents of some relatives closer together, others farther apart as their time on the road frayed nerves and brought long-standing resentments into the open. She remembered seeing a green tent near the edge of the camp the day before, and now it was closer to where others were pitched and another smaller tent had been added to one side of it, a sheep pen built nearby. It wasn't long until she found herself confused. She took a wrong turn, came up against a blockade of boulders, and had to double back the way she'd come. She sidled between a pen with two donkeys in it and a group of women at work on their looms.

And found Gideon blocking her path.

He was not breathing nearly as hard as she was.

His feet planted, his arms crossed over his broad chest, he looked as she imagined he did when he faced an enemy on the field of battle. Invincible. Invulnerable.

Except for the muscle that jumped just where his beard skimmed his jaw.

It was the first crack she'd seen in his stony exterior, and, realizing it, she smiled.

"I see you have come to your senses and have come to thank me," she said.

"Do you think so? I think first, I need to hear the whole story. Is it true?" he asked, not as if he disputed his sister's story but as if he found it so remarkable, he had to be certain. "You killed the snake? And saved Keziah?"

There was no use pretending humility. She raised her chin and looked him in the eye. "I did."

"Vipers are as deadly as they are cunning. Yet you dared to take a rock and—"

"It seemed the simplest way to dispatch the creature."

"Before it dispatched my sister."

"They are said to move very quickly when they attack."

"And this one might have just as easily turned on you."

She shrugged and didn't bother to explain. On the streets of Pithom, there were a thousand different ways to die. She had long ago made peace with every one of them. "It did not."

"Keziah is grateful. And I..." He cleared his throat. "I am too. I have met many a soldier who would not dare stand up to a viper."

She was not used to such praise or to the rush of heat that crawled into her cheeks. Her only defense to the feelings was to feign indifference. "So then, you are here to thank me."

He bowed to her. "I am. Thank you."

Such a simple gesture. Such simple words. Yet they tangled around Rana's heart. In an effort to go somewhere she could be alone and consider what her reaction meant, she stepped to Gideon's left.

He stepped to his right, stopping her. "Keziah and I, we are all that is left of my family. She can be..." When he struggled for the word, Rana supplied it.

"Fanciful."

A smile played across his face, and Rana suddenly found it hard to breathe and had to look down at the ground so she didn't betray the way her stomach swooped and her cheeks grew hotter still.

"I try my best not to discourage her whims," Gideon admitted. "At least not too much. After all, she will be a wife someday, and then she will have a husband to tend to and children to raise. Her responsibilities to her family will weigh her down. She should have a little freedom while she is young."

"Yet there is grain that needs grinding."

His expression twisted in a way that told her he remembered his callous reprimand to Keziah back at the tent. Though Rana suspected it didn't happen often, he looked repentant. He coughed. "There is. And we must eat."

"And she has a brother who needs his food cooked and his clothes cleaned. From what I have seen of the two of you and the tent you share, Keziah does that well enough."

He nodded.

"It seems to me she is getting all the practice she needs to be a good and hardworking wife. For her to take a stroll now and again is not such a bad thing."

When he chuckled, the sound reminded Rana of the roll of distant thunder. "You are right, of course. She is a good sister, and dear to me, as she was to our parents. Which is why, if there is some way I could show how much I appreciate what you did—"

Rana held up a hand to stop his words. "Your sister's friendship is repayment enough. Unless you will forbid it?"

"I can think of no better friend for my sister."

It was her turn to nod her thanks.

"But still." Gideon was not a man to give up so easily, and he went right on. "If you will allow it, I would like to meet with your family and tell them how impressed I am with your courage."

"I have no family." To Rana's surprise, the secret she'd been hiding all her life came easily. "And you are right about my name. It is Egyptian. I am not one of you Hebrews." Another secret. Out in the open. "I am Egyptian."

"Then how—"

"I was running from the Medjay. You might as well know it. I was avoiding them because they thought I stole something. Which is not to say they were right," she added with a snap in her voice and a look that dared him to dispute her version of things. "I somehow ended up in Goshen. It was nothing more than a twist of fate, but with all the confusion that morning, people coming and going, packing their things, filling their carts...well, it allowed me to leave the city unnoticed."

"A twist of fate. Do you think that is what it was?"

"Don't you?"

"You have seen that our God works in mysterious ways."

Rana thought of the pillar of fire. Of the pillar of cloud. Of the way the waters of the Red Sea parted, a wall to each side of the cart where she hid that night. This time when she moved forward, Gideon stepped aside to allow her to pass then walked along at her side, not saying anything at all while she spent a few moments thinking.

"And your God, do you suppose He wanted me here?" she finally asked him.

"Maybe He did, so that you might save Keziah's life. Maybe He did for other reasons."

"And He does not care"—she gave Gideon a sidelong look—"that I am Egyptian?"

"You have seen how wondrous and how good our God can be. He led us out of bondage. He made a way for us across the Red Sea. Day and night, He leads us through the wilderness. He welcomes all who believe in and honor Him."

"And you?"

The way his top lip lifted, she knew he wasn't sure what she meant. "Do I believe in our God? Of course!"

"What I meant was, do you care that I am an Egyptian?"

He didn't answer immediately, and Rana understood. It was Hebrew slave soldiers like Gideon who had been sent into battle at the front of the lines by the Egyptians, the first to fight. It was Hebrew slave soldiers who died for a country that wasn't theirs, in the name of gods they did not honor, for a pharaoh who kept their wives and their children enslaved.

"It does not matter if you care that I am Egyptian or not," she told him, even though deep down, she thought it really might. "At least it will not matter for long. I intend to return, you see."

"To Egypt?"

She nodded.

"But how—" She looked toward Gideon just in time to see his face light with the most amazing smile. It was broad and warm, and it made Rana think Keziah might be right; there was a great deal more to Gideon than the hard exterior he presented to the world.

He was still smiling—was it with disbelief at how foolish she was or with admiration at her determination?—when he stopped walking so he could turn to her. "That morning I found you near the water. That is why you had the donkey. You intended to leave."

"Little good it did me." Even now, admitting it, her mouth soured. She hated the taste of defeat. "A donkey cannot swim the Red Sea."

He pursed his lips, considering this. But not for long. "It seems that you were meant to stay here. With our people."

She shook her head as if that would help order her thoughts. "I do not belong here."

"Yet perhaps our God thinks otherwise."

"Do gods pay that much attention to people? I mean, people who are not as important as priests or pharaohs or generals?"

"Egyptian gods? I do not know. But our God, the One True God? Don't you see it all around you?" He motioned left and right, taking in the entire camp with the gesture. "God cares for each and every one of us. Otherwise, He would not have brought us out of Egypt. He would not be leading us to Canaan."

"Keziah believes all will be perfect there."

"And you do not."

"I believe..." The reality crawled over Rana's shoulders like the touch of a cold wind. "I am not sure I have ever seen a place that is perfect."

"Yet people can make it so. The right people."

Her smile came and went. "I have not seen many of those either."

"Perhaps you will let us...Keziah, our friends... Perhaps you will let us teach you differently?"

"I will not be here long enough for you to do that, I do not think."

"Yet while you are here, we could try." Another smile, one that flashed like a glint of sunlight and like the heat of the sun, warmed

Rana's heart. "Perhaps I too could show you the ways of our people and the ways of our God," Gideon said. "That is, if you do not think as little of me as my sister does."

Rana turned around and walked away, the better to hide her smile when she called to him over her shoulder. "I would be happy for you to show me the Hebrew ways." She wiped the smile from her face before she looked over her shoulder at him. "But I still think you are as senseless and stubborn as a donkey."

CHAPTER TEN

It was impossible for Rana to sleep. Not because the night air was so hot against her skin, it made her feel like she was bread baking in a stone oven. Or because the people in the tent nearest to where she made herself a nest of gathered blankets stayed up long into the night praying, their voices so loud, they must have wanted to make sure their God could clearly hear them. It wasn't the chirp of insects that kept her awake, either, or the sensation that gnawed her stomach and reminded her that, though she'd managed to snatch some bread from one nearby tent and a bite of meat from another for her nightly meal, it hadn't been nearly enough to satisfy her hunger.

It was something else. Something that made her insides feel as if they were fizzing and bubbling. For a moment or two, when the moon was at its highest and she stared, marveling at the way it shone so brightly when the rest of the world was dark, she wondered if the feelings sparkling through her had anything to do with the friendship she'd forged with Keziah. How refreshing it was to have a friend who expected nothing in return aside from conversation and companionship, someone she could talk to and laugh with! She knew that was at least part of the reason for her restlessness, her happiness. The whole of the reason, though…

Rana sat up and poked at the blankets, but no matter how much she rearranged them and fluffed them and patted them, she could not distract herself from what she knew to be the truth.

Gideon.

One moment, she found herself smiling. The next, she told herself she was a fool.

It was true that, when Gideon realized she was an Egyptian, he had not walked away from her, and he had not reported her to Moses and Aaron as an intruder in the camp. Not as far as she knew.

Yes, he appreciated what she'd done to save Keziah's life. Her actions had impressed him, even.

No, he had not seemed shocked, and certainly not surprised, when she confessed she'd been running from the Medjay.

Yes, he had a smile that warmed her down to her toes.

No, it did not mean anything.

Not anything at all.

Gideon was grateful. That's all it was. He was relieved his sister was unharmed. He was thankful Rana had acted quickly and decisively and killed the snake.

The tenderness of his smile was inconsequential.

These were the facts, and she knew it, and they should have comforted her and helped settle the silly feeling that fluttered through her when she pictured Gideon. They did not, and realizing they wouldn't, she gathered the blankets and returned them to the place she'd found them. With her brain so busy and her body abuzz, there was no use even trying to sleep.

The pillar that guided the Hebrews still glowed like a thousand suns there at the center of the camp. But here at its edges in the hour just before dawn, the wilderness lay in shadows as dark as *Duat*, that underworld place where Ammit, the Devourer of the Dead who had the forequarters of a lion, the hindquarters of a hippopotamus, and the head of a crocodile, waited to consume the hearts of sinners.

Sinners the likes of street thieves.

Rana groaned. What had these Hebrews done to her? Right and wrong. Sin and sinners. She'd never been bothered by such thoughts before she joined the exodus out of Egypt, and her conscience pricked. Before that very moment, she didn't know she had one.

Another shake of her shoulders brought her back to her senses, and she stepped into the darkness. Here, the stars shone like pinpricks of light against a sky as black as the kohl Keziah had applied to her eyes. No matter how much goodness and peace she found among these people, she reminded herself, they were strangers. No matter how appealing it might be to think of Gideon's smiles and the warmth that shimmered in his eyes, he was a Hebrew man who would always live according to the laws and the traditions of his people, a man who would take a Hebrew wife.

And Rana...

She drew in a long gulp of air and let it out slowly, steadying herself, breathing out her fantasies so they could scatter into the night and dissolve.

Rana vowed to do the only thing she could do—concentrate on gathering all she needed to stay at the oasis and wait for a caravan bound for Egypt.

No matter how many warm smiles invaded her dreams.

Her mind was made up, but her thoughts were interrupted by the low rumble of men's voices, their words punctuated by the bleat of sheep. Surprised she wasn't alone, Rana squinted into the darkness for a better look. She had the advantage of being at the top of a small misshapen hill and below her, she spied three men. One of the men was so thin, it would have been impossible to see him when he turned sideways if not for his white woolen tunic. The second, though dressed the same, was his opposite, tall and broad. The third man was short and as she watched, he hitch-stepped around an outcropping of stones.

There was something familiar about them, about seeing them in the dark, and with a start, Rana remembered the night she took the donkey intending to make her way back across the Red Sea. That night, too, she'd seen three men. Only then, they carried waterskins. These men were surrounded by sheep. The animals scampered and scurried, and the men positioned themselves along the edges of the flock so they could urge the sheep farther into the hill country that surrounded the camp.

It seemed an odd time for anyone other than a restless woman with wayward thoughts to be up and about, but that only proved Rana's point. She was not a Hebrew. She did not understand these people or their customs. And she certainly did not understand shepherds.

At least this time when she smiled, it was not because she was thinking of a certain handsome soldier.

Because she had nothing else to do and nowhere else to go, she watched until men and beasts disappeared into the hills and the baaing and bleating faded along with their shadowy forms. The deep silence they left behind reminded her that there were no more answers to be found in the darkness than there were near campfires, and at least in the camp, she might scrounge some food to silence her rumbling stomach.

She'd just turned to go back to camp when she saw yet another figure wearing a head covering and a long tunic coming from the other direction. A woman, and she held something large and bulky at her side.

Weeks ago, Rana would have darted into the darkness to hide. Now, she knew there was no use even trying. A Hebrew was a Hebrew. She would greet the woman and go on her way.

Except this Hebrew, she realized too late, was Leah, the spinner.

Leah caught sight of her and waved, climbing the steep path up the hill before Rana could even begin to look for an escape route. She arrived out of breath.

"Ah, my dinner guest." What little starlight there was shimmered in Leah's eyes. She had a large basket propped against her hip and she pressed her free hand to her heart. "I have looked for you in the camp a dozen times since the day we met and never once saw you. What are you doing out here in the dark?"

"What are you doing here?" Rana countered, her voice as sharp as it would have been back in Pithom if she found another street thief too close to a market stall Rana had her eye on. It was a rude response and Rana's conscience nudged her again; Leah did not deserve such disrespect. Not when she'd been so generous with her bread. Rana tried again. "What I mean is—"

"Why is an old woman out all by herself before the sun is even up? I understand. It is kind of you to care enough to ask." She fingered the fine scarf wound at her neck. It was colorless in the dim light, but in her head, Rana saw the colors as clearly as if the sun shone fully on them. Stripes of ochre and red, a thin band of blue. The scarf was soft and fine, and for a brief time, it had belonged to Rana.

They both knew it. Leah chose not to mention it.

"Before the sun comes up," she said, "when the world is still dark and so very quiet, that is when Eliana speaks to me."

As if she expected Leah's daughter might be lurking somewhere in the shadows, Rana flinched and looked all around. "But she cannot speak to you. She is—"

"Dead. Yes, do not worry. I am not lying to myself. I know full well my daughter is gone." Leah touched a gentle hand to Rana's arm. "What I mean, of course, is that I hear the whisper of her memory."

"And yet you smile."

"Do I? Am I?" When Leah realized she was, indeed, smiling, she threw back her head and laughed. "I miss her with all my heart, but yes, thinking about my girl does make me smile. She was a true and loyal servant of God, and she was a gifted artisan as well. How lucky the world was to have Eliana in it. Even for so short a time. I had hoped to see her marry. I had prayed to bounce her children on my knee. But that was not God's will. Her loss cut my heart into ribbons, but her memory… Ah, with every thought I have of her, my heart begins to stitch itself whole again."

Rana did her best to understand, yet she was confused. "How can you be so steady in your belief? This God of yours, He allowed your daughter to die. Are you not angry?"

Leah didn't need to think about it. "There are times I am angry when I make mistakes in my work because I am not paying attention to what I am supposed to be doing," she said. "My wool is too thin. My wool is too thick. Yes, that makes me angry. And I am sometimes angry when I dye my wool and the color is more muddy than clear, or when I burn the bread I am making because I am so busy spinning that I lose track of all time. Or when the wool I spin isn't as soft as I'd like it to be, yes, I admit, that sometimes makes me angry too. But angry at God? That would be impossible. God has a plan for all of us, and He knows what is best. It was God's will to take Eliana." She choked on sudden tears, coughed, offered a small, gentle smile. "You remind me of her."

"No." Rana backed away. "That is not possible."

"Why, because she was Hebrew and you are not?"

It was not the kohl still painted on her eyes or the rouge on her cheeks that gave Rana away. It was too dark for Leah to see those clearly. "You know."

"From the moment I set eyes on you."

"Yet you invited me into your tent. You fed me."

"Does our God not tell us we must welcome strangers? Besides..." She set the basket on the ground and stretched her arm, probably cramped from carrying it so long. "It is as I said, you remind me of Eliana. You are nearly the same age, you are as pretty as she was too, and you have the same determination she did."

"You cannot know that."

"But I can! I do. I know you have not come to my fire looking for a meal, and that tells me you are finding your food in other places. Taking it, I think, because you have no other choice. I understand, but I am not saying stealing is a good thing," she added, putting one hand up, palm toward Rana as if that might stop Rana from thinking she approved. "Perhaps you could use your nimble fingers for better things."

"Through the years, the talent has served me well."

"I am sure it has. If you had a family—"

"I do not."

"I know if you had people who loved you and cared for you, you wouldn't have needed to resort to stealing. But I also know"—she touched a finger to the scarf she wore—"a real thief would never have returned this to me."

"I have never been anything but a thief."

"Do you think so? Like Eliana, you are someone's daughter."

"Not that I remember."

"And you are a friend, I think."

She thought of Keziah. "Only recently."

"Then that at least is a start." Leah lifted the basket and repositioned it against her hip. "I am collecting wool." She tipped her basket and Rana saw the bits of fluffy wool in it. "I am taking advantage of the gifts the sheep left for me yesterday."

"I can…" Rana didn't wait for Leah to hand it over, she took the basket from her. "I will carry it for you."

Leah responded with a smile and got to work, moving through the stunted vegetation, using both hands to pluck at the bits and pieces of wool just as Keziah had done the day before. Unlike Keziah, who imagined the wool the fruit of a wondrous bush in Canaan, Leah waited until she had a handful of fluff then tossed it in the basket Rana held out to her.

The smooth motion of her work was hypnotic, like the movements of the snake charmers in the market, and Rana was caught in the magic of it. For a time, she followed Leah in silence, and it was in that silence and in Leah's company that her troubles and her worries melted away.

It wasn't until a thin line of brilliant orange light showed on the horizon that Leah spoke again. She deposited more wool in the basket, brushed off her hands, and gave Rana a careful look. "I will teach you to spin."

"Spinning is work for old women," Rana answered, then instantly wished she could call the words back. "I am not saying you are old, Leah, it is just—"

"But I am old." Laughing, Leah turned toward the rising sun and its glorious color touched her, painting the wrinkles at the corners of her eyes, glinting against the silver strands of hair that peeked from beneath her headscarf. "I am one of the lucky ones, you see. God has allowed me to grow old enough to watch our people go from bondage to freedom. If it is His will, He will allow me to grow even older still, so that I might be blessed to set foot in Canaan and rejoice with our people when we arrive." She glanced at Rana out of the corner of her eye. "You feel it, too, don't you? The heady happiness of freedom?"

Rather than answer, Rana plucked wool from the nearest bush and rolled it in her fingers.

For a moment Leah rested a gentle hand on her shoulder before she moved to the next bush. "It is not easy to learn new ways. But you will. You will see. God will provide. I think He has already provided for you."

Rana shook her head. As kind as Leah had been to her, as understanding and wise, this time, she was wrong. "I have always provided for myself."

Leah kept working. "Do you think it is an accident that you are here with us?"

"I think…" Rana yanked another bit of wool from where it had been caught and dropped it in the basket and thought about her time with the Hebrews. "Some of the people here, they have shared their food, even when I have not asked. Just as you did. And I think if I did ask, they would do it again, and happily."

Leah nodded.

"And I think I have found a place to sleep every night, and sometimes, blankets to cushion me. But that is no different from my life in Pithom. Food, water, a place to rest. I have always been canny enough to take care of myself, all on my own."

"On your own? Do you think so? Then we have more to teach you. We need to show you that God will always provide. He has already provided for you."

Before Rana stumbled into Goshen, she would have told Leah she was a fool. Now, Rana could not find the words. What had she said, she'd always found food, water, a place to rest? Was it possible the Hebrew God had been providing for her?

As if in answer to the questions tickling her brain, Leah looked over her shoulder at Rana. "You will come back to my tent with me when we are finished? I have bread and dates and plenty of fresh water. I will show you how to comb the wool so that I can spin it, then we'll come back again to search for wool after the shepherds have been this way this morning."

"They have already been through," Rana told her.

Leah turned to her, her eyes wide with wonder, her soft, round face screwed into a look of confusion. "In the dark? They would not be so careless. There are too many dangers in the dark. Wildcats and wolves. Jackals and hyenas."

"Yet I saw it myself." Rana looked over her shoulder, pointed. "They took the sheep up there, to the hills to graze before you came along."

"Then I will look the way they went and see if there is wool waiting for me." Leah stepped around Rana. "Are you coming with me?"

She didn't wait to see if Rana would.

And to Rana's own surprise, she didn't hesitate.

She followed Leah.

CHAPTER ELEVEN

"Your hands. They are softer than ever." Keziah removed the lotion pot from her cosmetic storage box, took Rana's hand, and began to apply the soothing ointment. She looked at Rana in wonder. "It has been two days since I have seen you, and your hands, they are still as soft and smooth as when last you were here. In this heat and with the air so dry, how did you manage such a miracle?"

Rana pulled her hands to her side. "It is nothing. Really."

"It is something." Not one to be put off, Keziah again took her hands. "Your skin feels softer even than my potions can make it. If you have learned a beauty secret, you must share it, Rana. It is what friends do."

"It is not a secret. It is lanolin."

"From sheep's wool?" Keziah laughed. "I should have known. It has that special silkiness to it that even my concoctions cannot rival." She put her head close to Rana's, and even though they were safely within the tent Keziah shared with Gideon and they were alone, she lowered her voice. "Did you thieve some wool? Or an entire pot of a spinner's lanolin?"

"You accuse me of stealing? Even before you know the story?" Rana's words cut through the air between them, and she stepped back, drew in a long breath, apologized, because there were sudden tears in Keziah's eyes, and though she had meant to defend herself, she'd never meant to hurt Keziah. "I am sorry. I did not mean to snap at you."

"And I should not have said what I said." A single tear slipped down Keziah's cheek. "It is just—"

"It is just that you are right." They were standing near the table, and Rana sank down on one of the cushions there. "Of course you think of me as a thief. Gideon told you? About how I eluded the Medjay back in Pithom?"

Keziah's face paled and she sat across from Rana. "I should not have brought it up. I should not have assumed—"

"You assumed correctly," Rana told her. "It is only natural to think everything I own I have stolen. I have been a thief all my life."

It seemed to Rana that Keziah did not know what to make of this confession. Working over her bottom lip with her top teeth, she thought it over before she said, "That makes no sense at all. You are a good person."

"Do you think so?" Though she could not explain why, Rana's voice clogged with emotion. "It is kind of you to say it, but it is simply not true."

Keziah harumphed. "It is true because I say it is true. Is that not how it works? I mean, when you are judging a person's worth? A person's character? We do not make these decisions about ourselves, others make them for us. You say you are not a good person, yet when I look at you, I see something else altogether."

"One time saving your life—"

"Is certainly important to me!" Keziah's sudden grin lit up the inside of the tent. "But that is not what I mean. What you did in killing the snake, yes, that showed that you are a good and brave person, but, Rana, you show your goodness in other ways too. You are here today, are you not?"

"I am here because you sought me out and invited me."

"Yes, you see, that proves it. I searched the camp for you and found you, and I asked you to come to my tent because I was feeling gloomy. Gideon, he has been gone for two whole days, training with the other soldiers, sleeping at their encampment, and I am terribly bored without him. I do not know how long he might be away, and I have no one to talk to. And now that you have come along, now I have you and we can gossip and laugh together. So you see, you are a good person because you are doing a good deed. You are keeping me company, and your company makes me happy."

"I had not thought of it that way," Rana admitted. "Are you sure something as simple as this qualifies as a good deed? Even when being with you makes me as happy as you being with me?"

"It is a good deed, and a friendship. We are like sisters, and that cheers us both. So, tell me, Sister, about the Medjay and how you eluded them. They are known for their ruthlessness. It must have been very frightening for you to know they were pursuing you."

Over the last weeks, Rana had tried not to think about that last day in Pithom, yet at the mention of it, she couldn't keep her heart from skipping a beat or her voice from shaking. It was exactly the way she felt not too many days before when she could have sworn she heard the rumble of the voice of Asim, the Medjay who'd pledged to end her life.

She swallowed hard. "You have not seen…" She felt the fool for even mentioning it. "Back in Marah, before the bitter water in the well turned sweet, there was a man who thought to talk the people into returning to Egypt, a small, slight man who called out to the people and asked them to follow him. Do you know him?"

Keziah squeezed her eyes shut for a minute, thinking, before she opened them again and shook her head. "I cannot say I do. But there are so many people here in the camp, it is impossible to know everyone."

This was true and Rana could not dispute it. "He might be…" Putting her fears into words made her heart skip a beat. "He might be with another man. A big man." Like the big man and the two smaller men Rana had seen together in the early hours, taking their sheep into the hills.

The memory slammed into Rana and before she even knew she had moved, she found herself clutching the edge of the table and heard her own quick, sharp intake of breath.

"What is it?" Keziah asked, her voice breathy with concern. "Does just thinking of the way the Medjay hunted you, does it make you so frightened?"

"It is not that. Not at all. It is simply…"

Simply, what?

At the same time Rana fought to gather her composure, she reminded herself she was being far too fanciful. Hadn't she told herself before? Hadn't she reminded herself there was no way Asim would be traveling with the Hebrews? Still, the thought of the three men, first at the Red Sea, then in the silence before dawn, seemed too similar and too purposeful to be coincidental.

Keziah reached across the table to give Rana's hand a squeeze and Rana flinched, startled from her thoughts. "I am sorry," Keziah said. "You came to keep me company and now you are thinking of something serious, something that makes your eyes dark with concern, and it is my fault. I should not have brought up what Gideon said about the Medjay, about what you did before you joined us here in the camp."

"It is my life, and I cannot pretend it did not happen," Rana confessed. "You will be happy to know I have not stolen anything for two whole days!"

Keziah laughed. "That is progress, indeed. But it does not explain the lanolin."

Rana had forgotten about the lanolin. Now that she'd admitted her thievery to Keziah, now that she'd declared that she was trying to change, there didn't seem to be any use in lying about the lanolin.

"Leah," she said. "Do you know her?"

"Our families have been great friends for many years. She is a dear. I was…" Keziah looked away. She cleared her throat. "I was a friend to Eliana, her daughter."

"A fine girl from what I have heard."

"She was, and there was talk…" Keziah paused, considering how much to say. But she was Keziah, after all, and sure to say whatever was on her mind. "There was a time our families talked about a marriage between Gideon and Eliana."

The news stabbed Rana's heart. It was a silly reaction, of course. At least that is what she told herself. Yet she could not help but picture what Leah had once told her, how Leah had hoped to bounce Eliana's babies on her knee. Eliana and Gideon's.

"Was he…" Rana wanted to know. She didn't want to know. She couldn't help but ask. "Was Gideon heartbroken at Eliana's death?"

"I truly was. But like I said, she was a friend. We seldom saw each other, as she worked as a spinner and I lived in the grand house of my master, but when she died, oh, how I missed her! There was a decency and kindness in Eliana that I have seen in few other people. As for Gideon…" Keziah sighed. "When Leah and our parents discussed the marriage, Gideon did what any dutiful son would do. He considered it. Carefully. In case you have not yet noticed, Gideon does everything carefully. And I think he would have obeyed our parents' wishes had Eliana not been killed. He was shocked when she died. That is for certain. He was angry that Eliana, or any of our people, were so misused as to suffer. He was sorry he could not fulfill the wishes of the families. But heartbroken? No, Gideon was not heartbroken. He may be a soldier and braver than any man who ever walked the earth, but he has a heart as big as the sky. If it was broken, I surely would have known."

"He did not love her, then?"

Why was it important to know what was clearly none of her business?

Rana didn't explain. Keziah didn't ask.

"Gideon loves being a soldier. He loves the Lord our God and is eager to do His bidding. He loves me in the way brothers do, sometimes tolerating me and other times being so frustrated by what I do and say, I think he wants to scream. He loved our parents. Surely." She closed her eyes and bowed her head. "He and Eliana had met only once or twice. They had hardly spoken over all the years. He would have made the perfect husband, of course," she added with a smile. "But it was impossible for Gideon to love a girl he barely knew. It is not in his heart to pledge himself like that."

It was a sobering thought, and sad, yet relief swept through Rana like a breeze off the Nile.

Keziah eyed her. "You are smiling."

Rana wiped the smile from her face. "I am not."

"Why?"

"Since I am not smiling, it does not matter why."

"You are not smiling now, but you were smiling. Are you happy my brother was not so hurt by Eliana's death? Or are you happy he was not in love with Eliana in the first place? Is that it?"

"It is not up to me to say I am happy or not happy about anything your brother does." Rana picked at a loose thread on her wool tunic. She set her shoulders, raised her chin. "Like Eliana, I hardly know him."

Keziah made a noise that made it seem as if she understood, as if she agreed. Yet Rana could not fail to notice the flicker of amusement in her eyes. It was best to change the subject.

"Leah has offered to teach me to spin," Rana told her friend. "Right now, I am only combing the wool to get the fibers straight and even and to rid it of any briars or bits of dirt."

Keziah puckered her lips; she'd clearly been hoping for more gossip and was disappointed the subject had been changed, but she recovered quickly enough. She clapped her hands. "That is wonderful news. Spinning is a valuable art. It will make you a prize on the marriage market."

"Keziah." Rana gave her a long look. No matter how hard she tried, Keziah would not get Rana back onto the subject of Gideon.

Instead, she reminded her friend of the reality of the situation. "No one here in the camp or in Canaan, or in any other place the Hebrews might be headed is going to want to marry an Egyptian. That is why—"

She might have gone on and confessed that she was planning to stay in Elim even when the Hebrews went on their way, but she didn't have the chance. The flap of the tent flicked open, and Gideon strode in.

"Brother!" Keziah jumped up to greet him. "I thought not to see you for a few more days yet."

Gideon's face was a thundercloud. Instead of saying anything at all, he unfastened his sword, slid his bow and the quiver of arrows from his shoulder. One corner of his mouth pulled into an expression that was either disappointment or self-contempt, he held out his left arm to reveal a cloth wound around it. It was soaked with blood.

"Oh, Gideon!" Keziah clapped her hands to her mouth and recoiled in horror.

"It is not as bad as it looks," he assured her, but Rana could not help but notice that when he attempted to unwind the cloth, he sucked in a sharp breath.

She rose and closed in on him. "Here, let me help."

She thought he might refuse. She was surprised when he didn't.

Carefully, she unraveled the rough woolen fabric. Beneath it was a cut as long as the stick Keziah had used to apply the kohl to Rana's eyes. Still bleeding. The wound needed tending.

"Surely soldiers know how to bind up each other's wounds. They could have taken care of this for you at the camp," Rana said, but no sooner were the words out of her mouth than she knew the truth. Perhaps she knew Gideon better than she thought she did. "You did this to yourself by some careless accident. And you did not want any of your fellow soldiers to know how clumsy you were."

"A stupid slip of a sword when I was grinding the blade," Gideon grumbled, clearly disgusted with himself. "I should have been paying more attention."

"And you are too manly to admit your error to your comrades." Rana couldn't help herself. Even as she wiped the blood on his arm, she smiled. "You came home to have it tended."

"I came home to look after it myself." He made to move his arm away, but Rana would have none of it. She held on to him, refused to let him budge.

"Two things," she said over her shoulder to Keziah. "Water and beer. You can get them for me?"

"Water, surely." Keziah moved toward the doorway of the tent. "But beer I am not so sure about. Our God does not approve of drunkenness."

"Which does not mean there is not any beer in the camp," Gideon told her. "Go to the tent of Asher, the man who knew our parents in Goshen, the one who has such a strong, clear singing voice. If I know Asher, he will have beer. In fact, you will probably find him making a new batch of it."

Keziah left, and Rana urged Gideon to sit. He actually listened, and before he could change his mind, she sat across from him, laid his arm on the table, and drew a lamp nearer for a closer look.

"You are lucky," she told him. "The cut is not so deep that it will allow evil spirits to enter your body."

He flashed her a look. "That is your religion, not mine."

"You mean—"

"We do not believe such things to be true."

As she thought this over, Rana wiped away more blood. "There is so much that is different between your world and mine."

"And so, you choose to believe in evil spirits, and I choose to believe in the power and goodness of my God."

While she turned the thought over in her head, she peered at the wound. "I have seen your God's goodness again and again. But when a person believes one thing all her life, it is difficult for her to look at the world in a different way."

He grunted his agreement.

"Which does not mean all my beliefs are contrary to what you might believe," she told him, because she thought he might need a reminder. "For instance—"

Keziah swept through the doorway and deposited a jug of water and a bowl on the table then was gone again.

"I know we need to get this wound cleaned up," Rana told him. There was a cloth on top of a basket nearby, and she took it and wetted it down. "The water is cool, and it might sting," she warned him.

She started with the undamaged skin around the cut that was caked with dry blood, slowly and carefully wiping it before she moved on to the wound itself. At the first touch of cloth to cut, Gideon gritted his teeth.

"It will take but a moment to finish," she assured him. "Just be sure to hold very still."

"You sound like a physician."

She thought it might be a compliment, and she wasn't sure how to handle a compliment. Not one coming from Gideon. She shrugged. "There are women physicians."

"Yes, but Egyptian physicians are trained by your priests and by other physicians. And you—"

"Learned all I needed on the streets." She rinsed the cloth, soaked it again. "You noticed this, the second time we met." She pushed up her left sleeve to show him the scar on her wrist.

His brows dropped low over his eyes. "Are you telling me you tended to that yourself?"

"I had little choice. You wonder how I know such medicine, and I can only say that, as a child, I learned what I had to learn. I had seen others bandage their wounds, and though I was young and did not attend to it as carefully as I promise to look after yours, my wound healed after a while. If I had done a better job of it..." She wrinkled her nose and studied the scar, and realized that these days, she barely paid it any mind. It was simply a part of who she was. "Well, if I had had a little more skill, I might not have a scar at all."

"Your wound was more serious than mine. I can tell just by looking at that scar. It was certainly deeper." His voice simmered with concern, and she was so caught by it, she did not notice when he moved, not until he touched his thumb to her scar.

Her breath caught. She had no choice but to make light of the whole thing. "The cut may have been deep, but I assure you, no evil spirits entered my body as a result."

"You know that is not what I meant."

"I do." She dipped her head.

She had no time to say anything else. Like a breeze, Keziah came back through the doorway. This time she carried a clay pot.

If Keziah noticed that her arrival caused Gideon to pull his hand away or that Rana sat back and drew in a stuttering breath, she didn't comment.

"Asher says to use as little of this beer as you can," she said, setting the pot on the table between them. "He says beer is too valuable to waste."

"I promise," Rana told her, and because she knew what was to come and wanted to get it over with as quickly as she could, she poured some of the beer into the bowl, and dunked her cloth.

"It is going to sting," she told Gideon.

"I know." He clenched his teeth.

"I cannot watch! I will wait outside and tend the fire." Keziah spun and hurried from the tent.

"I will be as gentle as I can," Rana told him.

He flashed her a smile. "Then let us get it over with."

She did, wiping the beer-soaked cloth over the wound, shutting out the sharp, quick intake of Gideon's breath so she wouldn't lose her nerve, telling herself she was doing what she had to do, not to hurt him but to help. It was only after she was finished that she dared to look up at him.

"Done," she told him.

He let go of the breath he'd been holding and made to move, but she would have none of that. Not yet. She put a hand to his to remind him to keep his place.

"Done with the cleaning, but you know I am not finished. Do you have honey?"

He poked his chin toward the far corner of the tent. "In one of those pots over there, I think. At least that is where it should be. Keziah is not known to always put things back in the place they came from."

Rana got up and peered into the first pot. It was filled with dates.

The second contained grain that would be ground and baked into bread.

When she opened the third, she told him, "Keziah is a loving sister to you." She took the pot of honey to the table. "She cares for your welfare."

"As do you."

"Not your welfare, just your wound," she told him, and hoped the smile she sent his way told him she was teasing.

She sat again, dipped two fingers in the honey, and being as gentle as she could, she coated the wound. "Let it dry to become a barrier to dirt and"—she swallowed what she had almost said—"then I will bandage it again. Only…" She glanced around the tent.

"If you are looking for cloth, there is plenty. Those big baskets over there are filled with it. Keziah!" he called, and she pushed back the flap and entered the tent. "Rana needs strips of wool."

"No, not wool," Rana told him. "Wool does not allow enough air to circulate over the wound, and that air is important for healing. We need linen."

Keziah shook her head. "We do not spin or weave linen. That is an Egyptian cloth."

"Yes, it is." If they wondered why Rana smiled, their curiosity was satisfied soon enough. Turning her back on Gideon, she lifted her woolen tunic just enough to reveal the linen tunic she wore beneath it. She started at the hem and ripped the fabric up then waved Keziah over.

"Here," she told Keziah. "Hang onto this piece of fabric, and when you do…"

When she did, Rana spun around and around, and when she was finished, a little light-headed from twirling, Keziah had a long strip of linen in her hand.

"Perfect," Rana said, and she went to the table to finish her work. When she had, she sat back, satisfied. "We will look at the wound every day," she told Gideon, "and wrap it with fresh linen if we need to."

When he smiled, the skin at the corners of his eyes crinkled. "If we do that, you will have no Egyptian clothing left."

"She will not need Egyptian clothing," Keziah informed him. "Rana is working with Leah. She is learning to spin wool."

The look he turned on Rana sparkled with admiration. "A worthy task for one with such nimble fingers."

"So Leah says." She rose from her cushion. She had best be on her way before the warm glow in his eyes turned her head. "And now, I should get back to her. We have been collecting bits of wool from the wilderness, and there's much to do."

"But you will stay and share a meal with us." Keziah did not say it as a question. To her, there was no doubt. "It is the least we can do to thank you for all your help."

As if it was a barrier to the kind words, Rana held up a hand. "I have heard that supplies are running low throughout the camp. It wouldn't be right to use yours. There will be plenty of bread around Leah's fire."

Gideon rose and joined her near the doorway. "Then let me thank you now," he said, and he bowed from the waist as he would if she were some grand lady, a person of importance rather than just a woman with nimble fingers and soft hands. "You are a true friend. Both to Keziah and to me."

There was nothing Rana could say. No words that would make their way past the sudden knot in her throat. Instead, she moved to the doorway, and Gideon stepped up behind her.

She pushed back the flap of fabric and caught her breath.

Here, the sky above the camp was as blue as lapis lazuli, and the air was calm. But there, on the horizon and moving nearer by the second, was a wall of brown air that roiled and rolled like a thundercloud and soared many times taller than the hills.

Gideon's hand clamped around Rana's arm, and he yanked her back into the tent and closed the flap at the same time he yelled, "Get cloths and soak them in water. Cover your nose and mouth. There is a sandstorm coming!"

CHAPTER TWELVE

"We are safe here, are we not?" Keziah's eyes were wide, her body rigid. She stood at the center of the tent, frozen with fear.

"Of course we are safe inside the tent." Gideon put an arm around her shoulders and led her to one of the cushions, and while he settled her, Rana did as he instructed. She found three cloths, soaked them with water, gave one to each of them, keeping one for herself, and they tied them around their faces so that their noses and mouths were covered.

"The sand is mixed with fine particles of dust," Gideon explained, his voice muffled, his beard bristling below the bottom of a cloth. "The cloths will make sure we do not breathe any of it in."

He urged Rana to sit on the cushion opposite Keziah and took a seat himself on the rug at the head of the table, Rana to his left and Keziah to his right.

Outside, all was calm.

"The storm has changed direction." Trying to convince herself, Keziah nodded. "See how quiet it is? It is not coming this way, is it? It is—"

A sudden gust made the tent shiver, and Keziah's words dissolved in a wail of panic equaled only by the howl of the wind outside.

"It is here!" Keziah grabbed Rana's hand.

Rana held on tight, and when another wind gust blasted through the tent and blew out the oil lamp on the table, they were plunged into darkness.

This was not a darkness like any Rana had ever seen. Not the blue black of night along the Nile. Or the gray she sometimes saw when night gathered above the far-away hills. It was not the starry darkness of the wilderness, either, that blackness relieved by the reassuring light of the pillar of fire. Now, the very air around them turned the color of mushrooms then darkened to a brown like a hyena's fur. She could not say how she knew, yet something deep in Rana's bones told her that was not the end of it. She held her breath. Only a moment later, the air turned the orange of an angry sunset shot through with a color as deep and as intense as Gideon's blood.

Keziah whimpered, the sound nearly lost beneath the roar of the wind and a sudden hammering against the tent. Grains of sand. Innumerable. Too tiny to do any damage, one by one, but with the full force of the wind behind it, the very desert itself rose into the air and slammed into the camp. "It will not last long, will it?"

Gideon covered her left hand with his right. "These storms, they can last for hours," he told his sister, and when she flinched, her eyes wide and suddenly filled with tears, he tightened his hold on her. "There is nothing to worry about. We are here together, and we are safe," he reminded her.

"But what if we were not?" Keziah's voice hiccupped over her words. "If you were with the other soldiers as you were supposed to have been, if I had not been able to locate Rana in the camp today, Brother, I would be all alone."

He gave her hand a squeeze. "But you are not."

"There is nothing to fear," Rana told her, though if she were honest with herself, she would admit her insides were jumping like a thousand grasshoppers and the pounding of her heart was every bit as furious as the drumming of the bits of sand against the tent. Rana reached for Keziah's right hand and held on tight. "Your brother is right. We are here together. That is the important thing. We have water should we need it. And beer." She laughed, not because there was anything funny about the situation but because she realized suddenly how lucky they were to be where they were and have what they had, to have each other, and the thought lightened her worries. If only she could see through the darkness to find it, she might pour herself a cup of beer! "There is nothing that can—"

An explosion of wind blew the drapery across the doorway into the tent then sucked it out again and took Rana's words with it. The cloth that served as a door tore in two, and sand shot through the tent. Propelled by the furious wind, it smacked into the baskets stacked around them and struck their hands and faces with what felt like the sting of a thousand insects.

Gideon did not waste a moment. He jumped from his seat, and because it was nearly impossible to see, he felt his way over to a basket in the corner, pulled out a large piece of cloth, and, fighting against the wind, made his way to the doorway with it. He tried his best to pin the new cloth over the doorway, to block the worst of the wind, but Rana knew from the start, with the force of the wind working against him and hampered by the wound to his arm, that was an impossible task.

She stood, holding one hand in front of her face to shield it from the battering sand. Her head bent and her shoulders hunched against the power of the wind, she fought her way to Gideon's side.

"Here." She grabbed one corner of the cloth, lost it when the wind snatched it out of her hand, scrambled to seize it again, and twisted it through her fingers. "I will hold it," she yelled, struggling to be heard over the shrieks of the wind. "You can fasten it in place."

Did he hear her?

She couldn't say, but Gideon knew what she was attempting to do. He tied one corner of the cloth in place, and she pretended not to hear it when he grunted from the pain of doing too much too soon with his left arm. If she were taller, if she had more strength, Rana would have taken over the task for him. But she was too small, too slight, and she did all she could, moving with him to the other side of the doorway. Before they could get there, the cloth she hung onto acted like a sail and would have swept Rana off her feet and into the murky air if Gideon hadn't hooked an arm around her waist and held her close to his side. When he was finished fastening the cloth, he dragged baskets from the corner and positioned them at the bottom of the cloth to hold it in place.

It was not perfect, but it would hold.

At least if the storm did not last too long. If it didn't get worse.

The look they exchanged above their cloth masks told them they both knew it and, as one, they turned away from the doorway. In the dark, it was hard to know where to step. The rust-colored air closed over Rana, smothering her like a hand over her mouth. It blinded her, disoriented her until she felt as if she were floating in a void. There was no earth, no sky. All was darkness and in the darkness, there was no up or down. She had no anchor.

Until Gideon took her hand.

He hung on tight and led her back to the table and the cushion she'd risen from so recently, already coated with coarse sand. Though it was fruitless to even try, Rana brushed the grit away before she sat down, and all the while, Gideon did not let go of her.

The air around them heated hotter than an oven and made breathing nearly impossible. Sweat beaded on Rana's forehead. It trickled down her back. The wind screamed, and the darkness, the red, red darkness, closed over them like a blanket. Rana groped along the table for the water jug she'd left there then motioned first to Keziah, then to Gideon, for their facecloths. Quickly, so that they wouldn't breathe in too much of the powdery dust that stung her eyes and blocked her ears, she rinsed each cloth and passed it back to them.

Keziah finished tying hers back in place. "The storm, it is not letting up," she whimpered.

"It will not," her brother told her, and though the news was disheartening his voice was firm. "Not for a while. And there is nothing..." He rumbled his annoyance. "There is nothing we can do but sit here and wait it out. Yet my comrades—" He glanced over his shoulder in the direction of the doorway. "They are still in the encampment and more exposed than we are. And the people of the camp, if any of them were caught outside their tents—"

"No," Rana told him, because she felt his muscles tense and knew he meant to spring up. She wound her fingers through his and saw the stain of blood against the linen she had wound around his arm; he'd done too much fixing the cloth over the tent opening and the wound had split open. She would need to clean and dress it again. "You cannot help them. Not while the storm rages. You would only get disoriented in the darkness, and then..." She wondered, with the damp cloth over her mouth, could he hear her pretended sigh of exasperation? "I, no doubt, would have to come rescue you."

"And then I would have to come after Rana and rescue you both," Keziah announced, distracted from the danger for a moment by Rana's jesting, just as Rana had intended. "And you know how I hate it when the wind blows my headscarf away and my hair gets mussed."

Their twin thoughts were like those of sisters, and their unspoken strategy worked. The tension went out of Gideon. He chuckled. "There is nothing a man can do. Not when the two of you oppose him."

"There is no opposition here," Rana pointed out. "Just common sense. Getting lost in the storm does no one any good."

Keziah said, "It is fearsome. Not like a storm, really, so much as chaos."

From the sound of her shaky breath, Rana knew it was time to try to turn Keziah's thoughts from danger again. Though it was the last thing she felt like doing, she laughed. "The world was created out of chaos. You know the story, do you not? How the god, Atum, existed in the water of Nu, which is another name for chaos. How Atum is the source of all the forces in the word? He gave rise to Shu, and that is the god of air, and to Shu's sister, Tefnut. They produced the earth god, Geb, and the sky god, Nut, and Geb and Nut had four children, and you surely know them. The great Osiris, and Isis, Set, and Nephthys. These are the gods who made all life possible. And you see, it all started with chaos. That is the story."

"A story, yes." Gideon's voice was as firm as the feel of his hand against Rana's. "But Keziah and I, our people, we do not need to listen to that story. You see, we know the truth. Yes, just like in the Egyptian story, we believe that in the beginning, the earth was without form. Darkness was upon the face of the deep. That is, until the spirit of God moved over the waters. And God said, 'Let there be light.'"

"And there was light." Keziah's voice was soft, humble.

In the eerie light, Rana saw Gideon nod, and listened as his voice changed. He was still the brave soldier. Still the loving brother. But he was reverent too. Respectful of his God, awed by His power. "God made the day and the night. He created the firmament that was heaven, and the dry land and the seas. He made all growing things, and so that there would be one great light to rule the day and another lesser light to rule the night, He created the sun and moon, and the stars too."

"And then the creatures of the earth." Rana didn't have to see Keziah's face clearly; she knew that behind her cloth mask, Keziah was smiling. "I love hearing about the creatures. The fowl and the fish, and then the cattle. And creeping things too." She gave her shoulder a shake. "Like that viper that nearly ended my life. At night, when I think about what nearly happened, I remind myself that the snake, too, was one of God's creatures."

"And God, He saw all this was good." Gideon took over the rest of the telling. "And then He made man in His image, male and female, He created them. And He saw everything He made, and He said it was all very good."

His voice was entrancing, his words thrilling, and when he finished speaking, Rana needed to call herself back from the spell they cast. Yet once his story was finished and the sound of the winds and the driving sand again filled her ears, she thought about it and said, "But do you not see, your story of the creation is not so different from mine. In both the stories, the world starts out of chaos."

Gideon barked out a laugh. "Yes, but after that, it took how many Egyptian gods to create the world?" He paused, remembering Rana's tale, counting. "Nine? Our God is the greater God, the only God. He did not need eight others to help Him. We must thank Him. For keeping us safe. Just as He did the night Death passed through Egypt and took with it all the firstborn."

The puzzle had nagged at Rana's mind. She remembered the night, the keening of the misery of the people of Pithom. She remembered their eyes red and swollen with tears the next morning. She remembered—she shivered in spite of the heat—the body of the man whose bed she'd hidden under when the Medjay searched for her. "So many were taken by Death, the Destroyer. But not the firstborn of the Hebrews."

"That is simple enough to explain," Gideon told her. "The Lord told Moses and Aaron to take a male lamb in its first year, to take a bunch of hyssop and dip it in the blood of the lamb. We used the hyssop to anoint our doorways with the blood of the lamb, and the Lord, when He saw our dwellings so marked, made it so that the Angel of Death passed over us."

Keziah gave Rana's hand a squeeze. "You are not firstborn in your family. You were spared."

It was not anything Rana had ever thought about. If she ever had a family, she had no memory of it. Yet she must have some older sibling—a brother or a sister—who had been taken by Death that terrible night.

She swallowed down tears. "Your God is fearsome," she said.

"And now, we should pray to Him as we did that night. Now, with this storm raging around us, we ask for His protection as we did then. We ask for blessing. For safety."

Gideon and Keziah bowed their heads, and because she didn't know what else to do, Rana did, too, and she cleared her mind and stilled her heart and listened when Gideon said, "Lay us down to sleep, Lord our God, in peace. Raise us, our King, to life. Spread over us the shelter of Your peace. Set us aright with the good counsel from before Your Presence and save us for Your Name's sake. Shield us, remove—"

A blast of wind, stronger than all the others, shook the tent and rattled the crockery. Keziah muffled a scream. Rana held onto her tighter. Gideon, his voice as firm and strong as his faith, prayed on.

"Shield us, remove from us foe, plague, sword, famine, and woe. And remove spiritual impediments from before us and from behind us and shelter us in the shadow of Your wings. For God who protects and rescues you." He tightened his hold on Rana's hand. "For God, the gracious and compassionate. Safeguard our going and coming. For life and for peace from now until eternity. Blessed are You, Lord, Guardian of the Twelve Tribes for always."

The storm still raged, yet peace washed over Rana. "Shelter us in the shadow of Your wings." The words for the prayer settled in her heart and calmed her mind and brought peace to her soul.

"Amen," Keziah said once Gideon's words had faded away.

"Amen," Rana whispered, and even though she did, she realized she could hear the word, not just in her mind and her heart. She heard the soft whisper of her own voice.

The storm had passed.

CHAPTER THIRTEEN

"You are not leaving this tent until I redress your wound."

Since Gideon was still holding onto Rana's hand, it wasn't hard for her to twine her fingers through his, to hang on tighter. She did, and refused to let go even when he stood and made to move toward the doorway.

"The people need me," he said.

"They need you alive," she reminded him. She shouldn't have had to. The linen bandage around his arm was soaked with blood, and they both knew the combination of an open wound and the dust still swirling in the air could have serious consequences.

"I am not worried about evil demons invading your body, if that is what you think," she told him. "From what I have seen of you, the demons would not have you. You would frighten them so, they would run in the other direction."

He had the boldness to smile. "You think so? Me? Frighten anyone or anything? I cannot imagine why you think that. I have actually been extra nice with you around."

"If your stubbornness is what extra nice looks like…" She tugged him so that he sat back down, but she didn't finish the sentence. She could not find the words. What she hoped to say was something clever and funny, something that would remind him she was her own woman and would not be intimidated by him. But her heart said something very different, something she could not put into words, not any words she dared to speak.

If this is what extra nice looked like—being there within the safety of Gideon's home, enjoying the feel of his hand in hers—she could relish it all her days.

She banished the thought. Erased her smile. Swallowed the words. She was better off keeping her hands busy and her mind still by concentrating on unwinding the linen wrapping on his arm. The fresh blood flowing from the wound mingled with the honey she'd spread over it and all of the sticky mess was caked with the fine, red grit that had so recently filled the air.

"It will need to be cleaned again," she told him.

He grumbled and, again, made to stand. "I do not have time for such things. I cannot leave my comrades out there when—"

"Do you think you are the only one eager to get outside and see how things stand in the camp?" Rana did not mean to snap, but she was worn thin from the last hours of worry and dread. The noise of the storm. Her concern for Keziah. The wound on Gideon's arm, the one she'd tried her best to heal and he'd done his best to aggravate again. Strange, she realized, throughout it all, that her own safety had not concerned her as much as these other things had.

She wadded the linen wrapping and tossed it on the table. "There are others besides you who are anxious to see what damage the storm has done, others who have people who care for them and—" Her voice clogged and tears sprang to her eyes.

"You act as if you are the only one who has duties and responsibilities, Brother. You should know better." Keziah brought over the water jug, and while she was at it, she gave her brother a sour look. "Rana is thinking of Leah. She has been staying with Leah, you see. Leah is teaching her to spin. Of course, Rana is eager to get back to her tent and make sure Leah was not injured by the storm. And yet, though she is eager to look in on Leah as quickly as she can, she chooses to stay here and care for you. Instead of being impatient and bad-tempered, perhaps you should offer Rana your thanks."

"No," was Gideon's only reply.

Rana's heart sank.

Keziah's mouth fell open. But just as she pulled in a breath, ready to reprimand her brother, Gideon patted Rana's hand. "First I need to say I am sorry," he said, and she saw the truth of what he said in the warmth in his eyes. "Once you accept my apology, then I will offer you my thanks."

Since it was impossible to be upset when he looked at her that way—his dark gaze soft and one corner of his mouth pulled into a small smile of regret—Rana merely nodded. She cleared the emotion from her throat before she spoke. "Let me finish quickly," she told him. "Then we can both be on our way."

As it turned out, that was not so easy a thing to do. Finding an unsoiled cloth to cleanse the wound was nearly impossible. The inside of the tent was speckled with sand and coated with the fine dust that had blasted through the air along with it. Even Keziah's baskets, sturdy though they were, were not made well enough to keep it out. Everything Keziah and Gideon owned—everything in the camp, Rana imagined—would need to be shaken and washed and aired.

Mumbling her displeasure, Keziah searched through their possessions, and Gideon grumbled, impatient. That is, until his sister finally let out a whoop of victory. "Here is one," Keziah said, pulling out a cloth from a basket and waving it over her head like a flag. "Folded inside another cloth, so as clean as can be."

"Perfect." When Keziah tossed the cloth, Rana caught it in one hand. She soaked the cloth with water and cleaned Gideon's arm, careful to wipe away every bit of the sand caught in the sticky honey.

"Are you really learning to spin?" he asked her while she worked.

She glanced up at him. "Spin? Well, that is what Leah calls it. Right now, I am not learning anything nearly as interesting as real spinning. You should see Leah's hands work over the wool! She turns it into thread like magic! As for me, I have spent these last days picking dirt and briars and sticks, and other unpleasant things"—she made a face—"out of the wool we gather and the wool brought to us by the shearers."

"Ah, the wool. That explains it. Why your hands are so soft."

She was surprised he noticed. Her hands stilled over her work, but not for long. Before the flattery could go to her head, Rana motioned to Keziah. "The beer!" Keziah brought it over, and after Rana wet the cloth with it and gently touched it to the wound, after Gideon sucked in a breath because the wound was still fresh and the beer stung, she lifted the jug and took a long drink, smiling at Gideon over the rim of the jug as she did. "You are right. Asher brews excellent beer."

"So I have heard," he said. Laughing, he took the jug from her, took a drink, and nodded his approval.

With Gideon's arm cleaned, the sand in her throat washed away by Asher's beer, Rana again spread honey over his injured skin, ripped more of her linen sheath into strips, and bound the wound. "There." She made a shooing motion toward the doorway. "Be on your way. Only, do not do too much lifting or carrying. You will aggravate the wound again. I will look at it again in a couple of days. Just to make sure it is healing properly."

He folded his right hand into a fist, laid it to his heart, and bowed.

A touching pledge, indeed. Except Rana didn't believe him. Not for an instant. Gideon was a man of honor and duty. Not to mention as obstinate as a mule. He would do what he had to do for his people, no matter the cost to himself. Heavy carrying and lifting were all part of his responsibilities.

At the same time she was telling herself there was nothing she could do about so annoying a man, her heart squeezed with something that felt less like admiration than it did affection.

"Come." He motioned to Rana and Keziah and stepped back to allow them outside ahead of him. Rana was only too glad to do as he asked. Better to get moving than to stand there with her thoughts running wild.

Outside, a new landscape greeted them, and seeing it, Rana's heart sank with shock then soared with relief. How lucky they'd been to come through the storm untouched! How sad that not everyone had fared so well.

A dozen or more tents that had stood nearby were blown down, the cloths that made up their walls and roofs scattered this way and that, their occupants, faces coated with grime, slowly gathering their possessions piece by piece. Every cooking fire was blown out, and clay ovens and the loaves of bread that had been baking in them were knocked on their sides, broken. What had once been a clearing with a large flat stone at the center of it was now a mound of sand taller than two men, and more sand was blown against carts and piled so deep on waterskins that only bits of them showed. Animal pens were destroyed, the flocks scattered.

"Casualties?" Gideon called out, and when none were reported, he motioned for the people to gather around. "We owe thanks to our God for bringing us through the storm."

There in a clearing that had previously held a tent, with broken crockery at their feet and torn fabric caught on rocks fluttering all around, they formed themselves into a large circle, and Rana imagined that throughout the camp, others did the same. In the close quarters shared by the brickmakers and the shared tents of the weavers and the larger, more comfortable quarters where the priests had their tents, shot through with threads of silver and gold. As one, the people gathered and bowed their heads.

"We give thanks to the Lord our God," Gideon said, and his voice was so clear and strong, it echoed against the faraway hills and shivered through Rana's blood. "Our God who has brought us through the storm. He is all-powerful, and good to His people. Amen."

"Amen," the people answered, and they stood silently for a minute until, one by one, they went on their way to pick through their windblown possessions and comfort their neighbors and hug each other close.

"I must go help," Keziah said, hurrying off in the direction of an old man and woman struggling to straighten the walls of their tent.

"And I must be off too," Gideon told Rana. "There will be much to do at the encampment. You will..." Gideon hesitated, as if choosing his words carefully. "You will come again?"

"I will. There is no use telling you not to do too much, so I will not even bother." She put a hand to his shoulder to turn him around and gave him a nudge on his way, and it wasn't until he was gone that she dared a prayer of her own.

"God of the Hebrews," she whispered, "You are mighty, indeed. You have brought Your people through the storm. You have brought me through the storm with them even though I am not one of them. May I ask a favor?" She lifted her eyes to the heavens where the sky was clear and as blue as if, in the story Gideon told her, it had just been created by their God. "It is Leah," she said, and worry clutched her, like a fist around her heart. "She has been kind to me. And she is teaching me to spin." She smiled at her own foolishness. Surely, any God who was great enough to protect them through such a storm already knew how she'd spent the last days, and it wasn't spinning! "I pray that she is safe. That she was not hurt. Please, I pray nothing happened to the beautiful scarf Eliana made her, for that would surely break her heart." She ended her prayer as she'd heard the Hebrews end theirs. "Amen," she said, before starting on her way. The storm may have changed the camp, but she still knew which direction to go and where Leah had pitched her tent.

She was almost there when she spotted Leah in the distance. Eliana's scarf was wrapped around her head.

"Thank You," Rana whispered with a glance toward the heavens, and when Leah waved to her, Rana waved back and hurried to meet her.

Leah looked her up and down. "You are not hurt?"

"You were protected?" Rana asked her at the same time, and when their questions overlapped, they laughed.

Leah nodded. "Protected by God. For He is great, and I have given Him my thanks."

"As I have too," Rana admitted, but as soon as the words were out of her mouth, she sucked in a breath. "Perhaps that was too insolent of me! I am only an Egyptian, and your God—"

"Is the God of all. Come." Leah put an arm around her shoulders. "So many of the animals were scattered in the storm. Come with me to the hills to look for them."

They were not the only ones scouring the wilderness around the camp. They passed shepherds carrying sheep to safety, and some leading rams by their horns back to their enclosures. Others were gathering bits of clothing and pieces of cloth, all of it tossed by the wind.

"We will come back this way another time for the wool," Leah explained, pointing toward a scraggly bush with wool tangled in its branches. "I think there is much we can collect. For now, it is more important for us to find the animals. Wool is one thing, eating is another. And if the flocks are gone..."

She didn't need to finish her thought. The prospect of losing the animals they depended on for food was a grim one, and while Leah went off to the left where the ground was less rocky, Rana went to the right and climbed a small hillock. From her vantage point, she could see all of the camp, and she gazed over it and gasped. Much had been destroyed, and all around the camp, she saw women shaking rugs and mats, ridding them of sand. Leah was concerned about the animals and rightly so, but Rana saw, too, that their water supply might have been spoiled by the storm. There were men gathered around the wells of Elim, looking down into the water, shrugging their shoulders, shaking their heads.

"It is a sobering sight, isn't it?"

The sound of a voice behind her brought Rana spinning around. She found herself looking at a man with flowing silvery hair and a bushy beard so long, it lay like a blanket against his broad chest. He was tall, dignified. His face was as wrinkled as an old blanket, and it was coated with dust so thick, it seemed as if he'd been carved from stone. His voice was as deep as one of the wells of Elim. She recognized that voice. This was the man she'd seen in Marah. She studied him, his great height, the breadth of his shoulders, the glint in his eyes. When she considered his age and how marvelous it was that he was still able to wrest a tree from the earth and toss it in the bitter water, she was awestruck.

"If there is much sand in the wells," the man said, "we will no longer be able to use the water."

And without the wells, caravans wouldn't stop at Elim, and without the caravans, it would be foolish for Rana to wait there, and if Rana didn't wait there...

The very thought hit her like a blow, and she sucked in a breath.

Without the chance of a caravan coming this way, she had no way to return to Egypt. She would need to go on. With Keziah and Leah. With Gideon.

She did not realize she was smiling until the man spoke again. "I see that you are not troubled by the prospect of the spoiled wells. You trust in the goodness of our God to provide for us."

"Well, no. Yes!" Rana was sure she looked like a fool, and she cringed. "What I mean is, of course I am worried about our water supply. We need fresh water. As do our animals. But if the wells here can no longer provide it for us, then we must move on."

He nodded. "To Canaan, yes. But we must have water to get there, don't you think?"

Why did she think he was testing her, waiting for her to give a wrong answer? Or was he perhaps hoping she would provide the right one?

She grasped her hands behind her back. "There is sure to be water in skins throughout the camp."

"And if it is enough for so many people, enough for many more days, that would be a good thing. But what if it is not?"

"You said it yourself. The goodness of our God will provide for us."

When the man laughed, the coating of dust on his face cracked, and his skin, browned from long days in the sun, showed through. "You have the quick mind of one of our priests or scholars. Yet I do not know you. Or your people, I do not think. What is your name?"

Did she dare reveal the secret to a stranger? The kindheartedness that glowed in his eyes convinced her. "Rana," she told him, and before he could question it, she added, "Yes, it is an Egyptian name."

He pursed his lips, nodded. "You are not ashamed of that, are you?"

"Not ashamed. Simply..." Because she could not explain, she shrugged. "I saw what happened to the Egyptians at the Red Sea, the soldiers, the charioteers." She shivered.

He narrowed his eyes and studied her carefully. "And so, you fear for your life."

"I did at first but not any longer. What I have discovered here"—she swept out an arm, taking in the entire camp—"everyone has been kind to me."

"And yet you hide your true self."

"I have heard the stories," she said. "About how the Egyptians enslaved the Hebrew people for hundreds of years. How the Hebrews were mistreated and many of them suffered and were killed. How your God was not recognized by the Egyptian pharaohs. So you see, I think I am not hiding my true self as much as I am ashamed. I am sorry for all my people did to yours."

"That is a wise thing for you to say."

It was Rana's turn to laugh. "Oh, no! I am not at all wise. I am just someone who needed a place to hide. I found my place. Here."

"The people here, they have accepted you?"

"Yes."

"As they have accepted me." When she looked at him in wonder, he smiled. "You see, I was raised in a fine Egyptian home, the finest, raised by royal Egyptians who had Hebrew slaves to do their every bidding. And so it is only natural that I have an Egyptian name too. It is Moses."

"No." Rana stepped back, shaking her head. "You cannot be Moses. Moses is not an old man with a white beard. Moses is a god!"

He screwed up his face, and bits of dried dust dropped from it and rained down on the ground. "Who told you that nonsense?"

"Well, no one," she admitted. "But the way the people talk about you, about the plagues you brought down on Egypt and—"

"I did nothing but follow the commands of our God."

"And the way you led the people from bondage."

"Again." He dipped his head. "I did only what my Lord asked of me."

"And you are the one who threw the tree in the well and used your magic to turn bitter water to sweet."

This time, he didn't say a thing. He simply pointed one finger toward the heavens.

Heat shot through Rana's cheeks. "I see I have a great deal to learn."

"As did I when I left my life in Pharaoh's court and joined with the people of my heritage. You will learn in time. Just as I did. For now, though, I think we must worry more about the lambs that are lost."

"And you are out here finding them? Do you not have servants to do these things for you?"

"I am the servant of God. As for the lambs…" He put his fists on his hips and looked all around, scanning the horizon, hoping to spy the animals. "I myself was a shepherd. The father of my wife is Jethro, a priest of Midian, and for many years, I tended his flocks."

"And then you freed the Hebrews from Egypt."

His shoulders rose in what was almost a shrug. "There are many flocks. And many sheep. And many"—he gave her a careful look—"are called to tend them."

"Even those who are Egyptians?"

Moses smiled. "Especially those who are Egyptians. For by doing His work, we show God that He is One and we are One with Him."

It seemed too deep a concept for a street thief to understand, yet Rana did her best to wrap her brain around it. She bid goodbye to

Moses and went on her way, promising herself she would think about all he said someday. Right now, she had more important things to worry about. Nightfall was closing in, and once it was dark, their animals would be in danger. There were predators in the wilderness.

Predators such as—

Not far from the camp and discouraged by her lack of success, Rana rounded a large standing boulder and stopped in her tracks.

There were two men there. One of them was as thin as a reed, and the other, when he stepped her way, dragged his leg. But it was not the men who surprised her as much as what they were doing. There were waterskins on the ground around them, and they were taking them, one by one, and storing them in hollows between the rocks.

Rana hurried forward. "No! What are you doing, you fools! If you hide the water supply, you destroy the herds. You destroy the people."

The men stopped what they were doing, but they didn't say a word. They simply looked past Rana, and it was that which should have served as a warning to her. Despite what Moses said, she wasn't clever at all, at least not clever enough to realize what was going on. She wasn't fast enough, either, to move even when she heard footsteps behind her.

The next thing she knew, an arm caught her around the throat, a hand clamped over her mouth, a voice growled in her ear. The voice of Asim the Medjay.

"Well, if it is not the little thief!"

CHAPTER FOURTEEN

Rana's heart felt as if it would burst from her chest. Her limbs froze. Her breath, trapped behind Asim's crushing grip, caught in her throat and choked her. She didn't have the time to wonder what Asim was doing there, or to question why he and the other two men had so many waterskins and so were endangering the lives of every man, woman, and child in the camp. There was no time to think about anything, especially the panic that gripped her.

There was only time to fight back.

Squirming in Asim's powerful grasp, she managed to raise her right foot. She brought it down hard on top of his, and when he yelped and loosened his hold ever so slightly, she slipped from under his arm and took off running.

This was no race like the one she'd led Asim on through Pithom. There the streets were smooth, and she knew every one of them. She had hiding places in every one of them too. A spot that was too small to accommodate the other street thieves there between a fountain and a stand of tall palm trees outside the temple of Tum, the god of the setting sun. Another place, shady and out of the way, at the back of the market stall maintained by a young man who was always willing to look the other way because he was beguiled by Rana's smile. At one time, there was the home of Zoser as well, the dog who had betrayed her to the Medjay, and if there was enough moisture in her mouth, Rana would have spat on the ground in his memory.

Here, even before the storm had changed the terrain, all was unfamiliar, and with the long shadows of evening gathering between the rocks and in the small crevices around the scrubby vegetation, the landscape was foreboding. There was no safety here. No comfort. No relief. There was no protection.

Except what she could depend upon from the people of the camp.

The very thought brought tears to her eyes, and this time when Rana's heart felt as if it would burst, it was from gratitude. She had friends in the camp. People who cared for her. She knew she would find shelter there.

If she could get to the camp before Asim and the other two men caught up to her.

She could ill afford a moment to pause, but there between an outcropping of stone and a mound of windblown sand, she stopped to try and get her bearings. A false move would take her farther into the wilderness, farther from safety. But which way should she go to get back to the camp? Were the men really as close behind her as their voices and footfalls warned?

Not all of them, she found out soon enough, when she decided to go to her right, skirted a boulder, and found the man with the lame leg there waiting to ambush her. He shuffled toward her, his arms stretched out to grab her, his fingers curled into claws like a falcon's. Keeping well away from his grasp, Rana stooped, grabbed a rock, and before he could call out to his comrades that he'd found their prize, she attacked. This was no snake she could crush with one blow, and she didn't even try. She ran at him, quick and low, and slammed the rock into his lame leg. His face twisted and he collapsed into the dirt, and while he thrashed in pain, she leaped over him and kept running, the rock still clutched in her hand.

Her throat was parched, her legs felt as if they were weighed down with stones. She remembered Moses, how broad and powerful he was. She wondered if he might still be somewhere nearby and thought about calling out to him for help. She didn't dare take the chance. If Asim heard her, he would easily find her.

Still running at breakneck speed, she skidded down a small hillock, kicking up a shower of dirt and pebbles as she did, and it wasn't until she was finally on level ground that she dared to glance over her shoulder to see if her pursuers were close behind. What she saw instead made her heart sink. It was the pillar above the camp, and even as she watched, it changed from cloud to fire. She berated herself. She was headed in the wrong direction.

She had no choice but to double back. She spun around. And slammed into Asim.

He was far larger. He wasn't breathing nearly as hard. He had a long, thin knife in his right hand. Rana jumped back, but there was no use trying to run. The other man, the skinny one, was right behind her and he, too, held a knife.

"So, little thief." Asim looked her up and down, the smile of a hyena on his face. "You wish to make this difficult on yourself. You would do better to keep still." He took a step toward her, and the blade of his knife flashed in the last rays of the day's sun. "That is, if you know what is good for you."

Rana narrowed her eyes, raised her chin. "I do," she told him, and raised her hand, ready to throw the rock.

She never had a chance. The man behind her seized her around the waist, knocking her back. Her feet skidded on the sandy ground, and she nearly went down, and while he had the advantage and the other man held onto her, Asim closed in on her, his eyes glinting, his knife raised.

He didn't use it. He didn't need to. Before she could prepare herself, he struck Rana across the face with the back of his hand. Her head snapped back. Her vision blurred. Her body sagged. The world around her burst into stars as bright as any she'd ever seen in the skies over Egypt. Then it faded completely to black.

When Rana regained her senses, the sky was dark. The stars were not as dazzling as the ones she'd seen when Asim's hand connected with her cheek. They twinkled, gently and steadily. It was peaceful. Quiet.

That is, except for the sounds of the three men talking in low voices.

The awareness brought her fully awake, and Rana sat up and gasped. She had no memory of falling to the ground, but now she found herself in the dirt at the base of a large rock. Asim and his two friends stood not far away. They were surrounded by waterskins.

Rana could only imagine how cool the water was, how refreshing. She ran her tongue over her lips. "What are you doing? What will the people in camp have to drink if you have all the waterskins?"

There was a sputtering fire burning nearby, and Asim stepped into the halo of light, a water jug in one hand. He slung the jug over his shoulder, threw back his head, and took a long drink. He smacked his lips and poured out even more water so that it dribbled down his neck and over his broad chest. "I would be a fool, indeed, if I took all the skins all at once. Then, surely, someone might notice. But one here, one there..." He strolled to where she sat, squatted so they were face to face. This close, she could see the light reflected in the drops of water along his neck. The orange glow of it reminded her of the way the day's last light had glinted on his knife. Like that knife, there was a deadly sharpness in his voice. "And I am no fool."

An idea slammed into her, as powerful as the force of Asim's slap. "You wish the Hebrew people to die out here in the wilderness."

"Hardly." He made to stand, changed his mind, held out the water jug to her. "Drink?" he asked.

Her tongue was swollen. Her mouth was dry. She wanted water more than she wanted her next breath. "No," she told him.

"More for me." He stood and poured water over his head, and Rana was grateful that he laughed while he did it, for then he didn't notice the way she darted out her tongue to catch whatever wayward drops of water splashed on her lips and chin. There were not nearly enough of them, and she savored each one like a taste of the divine. Those few drops gave her courage.

"I saw you," she told him. "Soon after we crossed the Red Sea. I thought you were Hebrews going to replenish the waterskins."

He looked down at her. "And now what do you think?"

"I think you were not filling the skins, you were emptying them."

"If a street thief was a little wiser"—he nudged her with the toe of his sandal—"she would have known from the start that we could not have been refilling the skins. Seawater has salt in it. Like that which is used to preserve fish. A smarter woman would know this. A stupid street thief?" He shrugged away the thought, and Rana scolded herself. The only body of water she'd ever seen before the night they crossed the Red Sea was the sacred Nile. She had no idea any water could taste of salt. If she had, she might have warned someone. She might have told Gideon, who was right there, accusing her of stealing a donkey.

At the image of him that popped into her mind, her heart squeezed, but she refused to let the tears that pooled in her eyes fall. She bit her bottom lip hard enough to draw blood. Better pain than admitting to weakness.

"And just recently, I saw you again. All three of you." Her gaze raked the other men, sitting at the fire. The man with the lame leg had a wet cloth on it, and when he looked at her, his eyes flashed with anger. "I thought you were shepherds, leading sheep into the hills to graze. But they were not your sheep. You stole them."

When he smiled, Asim's teeth glinted in the light. "Their meat was delicious. We roasted it with herbs."

Just the mention of food made Rana's stomach rumble, but she told herself her discomfort was of little concern. Not when there were more pressing things to worry about. "You do all this, and so the people suffer."

"The people!" Asim's laugh reminded her of stone grinding metal. "They are not people, not *our* people. They are Hebrews. And you are not one of them. Do I need to remind you?"

"They have been kind to me." Her voice was so small, she thought he could not have heard, but he did. That would explain why he pointed a finger at her, why he shuffled his feet in the sand as if a firmer stance, a stronger posture, would make her see that she was too inferior to know reason.

"They have been kind to her." Asim's words were mocking, and the other two men laughed. "And you are dressed as one of them." He scraped a look over her woolen tunic, her headscarf. "They do not know you are an Egyptian, do they?"

"You are dressed as they are too," she countered. "But then, that is what spies do. They do their best to blend in. They try to pretend they are no different. But you are different. You are evil. What you are attempting to do—"

"I am *attempting*..." He put a sour spin on the word and rid himself of the taste of it by spitting on the ground. "What we are doing, we are doing for the good of those you call the people."

"Starving them? Making them desperate for water? And you have been doing this for the whole time we have traveled, have you not? It must have galled you when we arrived at Elim. When you saw there was water aplenty and luscious dates on the trees. It is harder to starve people when they have supplies at hand."

"Not any longer. The wells are fouled. The trees are blown down, their fruit scattered. And all of it thanks to the storm."

He was right, and Rana hated him for it.

"You know about Set?" he asked.

She did, her heart sank.

Asim threw out his arms and his voice rang against the rocks. "Set, the god of chaos. Chaos, like that of the storm that overtook the camp."

"But not the True God," Rana told him.

"Oh, no." He wagged a finger at her. "I have heard enough of that jabber in the camp. All that talk of one God. All that talk of how He saves His people."

"How else do you explain their release from captivity? You might believe in Set, but did he or any of the Egyptian gods save the firstborn from dying back in Egypt?"

The way Asim came at her, she thought he would strike her again, and Rana braced herself for the blow. His hand near enough to her face for her to feel the heat from it, he stopped himself and patted her cheek.

She cringed at the touch. She would have preferred his fist to the touch of his hand.

"The God of the Hebrews can no longer save His people, though, can He? Do you see Him sending water? Do you see Him raining food down on the poor simpletons who trust in Him?"

"So, you will sit here with your water and your roasted lamb, and watch them die?"

"No. Not watch them die. That is not my mission."

Try as she might, she could make no sense of this, and the way her brows dipped low over her eyes must have told him as much.

"There were many slaves in Egypt," Asim said.

That was undeniable. She nodded.

"And now, those slaves have gone on this fool's journey with the bigger fool, Moses, and—"

"There is no one left to do the work." Rana couldn't help but smile. "All those hundreds of years, the Hebrews tended the farmlands and reared the Egyptians' children. All those years, they cooked the food and washed the clothes and made the bricks that built Pharaoh's cities, his palaces, the temples to the gods. And now..." Picturing it, she laughed out loud. "The Egyptians must now toil in the fields and make their own mud bricks. Oh, how the mighty must chafe at this new reality!"

"As I do at my new reality." Asim stalked to the fire, spun around, and came back at her. "I am tasked with living in this god-forsaken desert until I bring the slaves back with me."

"It is just as the thin man said at Marah!" Rana looked past Asim and to the man, sitting satisfied by the fire. "If there is no food and no water, the people might be anxious to return to Egypt, and then Pharaoh will have his slaves back. Egypt will have her workers."

"And I will have my pride again," Asim grunted. "You see, little thief, I am not trying to hurt your precious Hebrews. I am trying to help them. If they are desperate enough, they will return to Egypt with me. Then they will have food to eat, and the Nile will provide them with water."

"And they will be under the thumbs of the overseers again. They will be beaten and abused. They will be forced to make bricks without straw, to watch their families torn apart, and their God mocked." She wasn't sure her legs would hold her, but Rana put one hand against the nearby rock and pulled herself to her feet. She threw back her shoulders. "They will not go with you."

"They will. Oh yes, they will if they are hungry enough. I can save them with the water I have hidden along the way." He gave her a long look. "I can save you, too, and take you with me."

She thought of all the nights she'd dreamed of returning to Egypt. Of all the days she'd spent feeling alone even in the company of so many. She thought of her plan to stay in Elim, to wait for an opportunity very much like this. And her heart soared.

But only for a second.

The next moment, it beat with the certainty of truth.

"I do not wish to be saved," she told Asim. "Not by the likes of you."

If he was surprised by her declaration, he didn't show it. He pursed his lips, considering. "Food. Water. We have it all. And soon, we will have the people too. Perhaps not all of them, but most, I think, will abandon Moses and come with us. And you, little thief, could have a place of honor among them. You are tired of trudging through the heat?"

Though he waited for an answer, she didn't give him one, and Asim grunted. "The sun beats down on you day after day, and I know you are hot and weary, just as I know your stomach grumbles. I know what you will never admit. That you lie awake at night and ask yourself how you got into this mess, and how you can get out of it. And now, I am offering you the chance. Think about it. The streets of Pithom are inviting compared to this wasteland. And yet, if you come with me, you will never have to live on those streets again. You will be respected. You will be rewarded by Pharaoh himself. And all you need to do, little thief, is the exact thing you have done all your life. Steal. It is second nature to a woman such as you. All you have to do to assure a life of luxury from this day forward is to help us."

The outrage that shot through her was so strong, Rana could not speak. She turned her back on Asim. She waved a hand behind her, a way of telling him that he was mad and she would no longer stand there and listen. She was going back to camp.

Holding her breath, waiting for him to seize her, she walked away.

That is, until Asim spoke.

"Returning to the tent of the spinner, are you?"

Simple words. Yet they held her in place like a magician's evil spell.

She closed her eyes, curled her hands into fists at her sides, prayed for strength and found it in a small breeze that caressed her cheek.

When she turned again to Asim, her chin was high and her voice was steady. "What do you know of the spinner?"

"The spinner. And that young girl who never stops talking." He curled his top lip. "Yes, even the soldier. I have seen you with all of them."

"It means nothing." She shrugged because she knew, all too well, that it did *not* mean nothing. It meant something, something important and essential, something even more dear to her than her own life. It meant everything, and she couldn't let him know it. "I speak with many people in camp. I have to get to know them so I know their comings and goings. So I might raid their food supplies and steal their clothing." She touched a hand to her tunic. "Yes, the spinner and the girl. I have talked to them both. They mean no more to me than you do."

"Good. Then you will not care if one of them dies."

His statement was like a fist to her heart, and Rana doubled over. The next thing she knew, she was looking at Asim's sandals. He had come to stand in front of her.

She forced herself to stand upright, but she couldn't keep her voice from shaking. "You would not."

"Of course I would." There was no amusement in his laugh. "Surely you know that much about me by now, little thief. I have no special hatred for any of these people. Other than they are Hebrews. I do care that there are only three of us and we cannot work quickly enough to take as many supplies from the camp as we would like. And I would like to work quickly. Oh yes, I would like to get this infernal trek over with and return to Egypt with the Hebrews trailing behind me. Then I will be treated like a prince! And that is why I care about you." He crooked a finger under her chin and turned her face up to him. "You will help us."

She swallowed hard, but her tongue refused to form the words she needed.

"No matter, then." He dropped his hand, backed away, made a shooing motion. "You are free to leave us. Go! Back to the camp. Back to your friends. Only when you get there…" Cooly and calmly, he reached into his tunic and withdrew a long piece of cloth. In the low light, Rana thought her eyes must surely be playing tricks on her.

But she knew they were not.

She saw the ochre stripe on the scarf. The red. The band of blue.

And her throat clutched, and her breaths hung suspended on what felt to be a knife's edge sharper and more deadly even than Asim's weapon.

"Where did you get that?" She meant to sound demanding, but her voice trembled over the words. "How did you—"

"You do not think this friend of yours, you do not think she gave this trifle to me?"

"I do not think she would give it to a snake such as yourself."

"You are correct, of course." He stuffed Leah's beautiful scarf back into this tunic. "I told her she may get it back. Someday. Just as you may get her back. Someday. If you cooperate."

The words spun through Rana's head.

Get Leah back?

She wanted to ask what he meant. She wanted to know what he had done with Leah. She could not speak.

Instead, she whirled around. She would find Leah. She would tell Gideon of the threat to her. She would help. In whatever way she could.

But before she'd gone three steps, Asim's voice trembled in the air between them. "You won't find her there in camp. The spinner lady. I have…removed her to another place."

"If you have harmed her…" Before she even knew she'd moved, Rana had raced forward. Her hands balled into fists, she beat at Asim's chest.

He was a large man, and he took her shoulders in his crushing grip and held her at arm's length. "She is not hurt," he growled. "Not yet."

The anger drained from Rana. It was replaced by a terror that left her limp. All her life, she knew it would take more than the waters of the mighty Nile turning into blood to frighten her. More than locusts, or hail and fire raining down from the sky. Fear? She had never in her life felt real fear.

Until that very moment.

CHAPTER FIFTEEN

There were no cool breezes. No dates high up in palm trees, the sweet fruit glistening in the sun. In fact, there were no palm trees at all. There were no wells for water. No boulders large enough to provide even a sliver of shade for a multitude. The only relief from the searing sun was found inside tents, but even there, the air sat hot and still. Like the inside of a tomb.

It was impossible to imagine a place more desolate than all the places they'd already traveled, yet on the day after she encountered Asim and they left Elim, the Hebrews camped in the region called the Wilderness of Sin, and one burning day followed another. It was a useless mission, Rana told herself time and again, yet over those days, she often found herself searching the skies, desperate to catch a glimpse of even a wisp of a cloud. Instead, the only thing she saw high, high above her in a sky so blue it hurt her eyes to look at it, were black specks. Vultures circling.

Not for the first time in the days since she'd encountered Asim, she wished the birds would swoop down and carry her off.

The thought weighed on her, as real as the worry for Leah that ate at her insides, as stifling as the heat that made it difficult to breathe, and she forced herself to look away from the birds, to finish what she'd come to do. She had no time to spare.

She was outside the tents of the potters at a place where they stored their waterskins, and, certain all were busy and none were watching, she lifted a skin and slung it over her shoulder. It made no difference how many times she'd done this. Her hands still shook as much as they had the first time. Her fingers were still slick against the skin. As if there was a wild animal inside her, ripping her apart, her stomach still clutched, and she felt as if she was going to be sick. She swallowed down the sourness in her mouth. Her breaths coming in quick, sharp gasps, she hurried away before anyone saw her, back toward the hills where Asim and his loathsome friends hid like the rats in the alleys of Pithom.

"You will tell no one about your friend, not if you wish to see her live. And you will turn the waterskins over to me." The memory of Asim's words and his breath, hot against her ear, crawled up her spine. *"Four skins every day without fail. More, if you wish to make sure your spinner friend does not spend too long in a place far less comfortable than her tent. It should be easy enough for you to accomplish this. You are nothing more than a thief."*

With no other choice, she did as she was told, and each time she approached the encampment where Asim and his men concealed themselves, each time as she left to return to the camp, she looked for a clue—any clue—that would tell her where they were keeping Leah. Only then, when she was sure Leah could be rescued quickly, would she dare to ask for help.

"I will kill her, you know." She did not need the memory of Asim's words to remind her. *"If I see anyone looking for her. If I hear anyone talking about searching for her. It will take me far less time to get to her than it will for you to find her. And by the time you do…"*

He had shrugged then, as if the thought of what would happen to Leah was nothing. As if the pain that ripped through Rana was little more than an inconvenience. He had hurried her on, back to her work.

"Four skins," Asim reminded her. "The thirstier the Hebrews are, the more likely they will want to return to Egypt. And when they do, when they have finally had enough of the sun and the heat and this endless wasteland, I will gather them up, and we will follow the same route we took to get to this forsaken place, and along the way, I will produce water for them from where I have hidden it. Oh, it will be wondrous! Better even than what Moses did at Elim. And they will be so grateful, I will be their god and they will do my bidding, and we will arrive back in Egypt, where they will proclaim my glory to Pharaoh!"

Remembering the look in his eyes made her shiver, but Rana could not let that stop her. She slipped away as only a thief could, and got lost in the crowd of Hebrews who went about their daily business, more desperate for food and water with each passing day, and no one paid her any mind. She was just a woman. A Hebrew woman. Perhaps she was carrying water to her family, perhaps she was taking it from here to there to share it with friends, and shame ate at her all the way to where Asim waited, and all the way back to camp.

By the time she arrived there, tears blurred her vision, or otherwise she would have seen Keziah approaching through the crowd, and by the time she did, Keziah already caught sight of her. She closed in, a smile on her face.

It was simple enough for a thief who had spent a lifetime hiding her emotions to dash the tears from her cheeks and wave back. To smile, though? Rana didn't even try.

"There you are!" Even Keziah, for all her youth and beauty, looked more worn-out each time she saw her. Her woolen tunic hung lower over her shoulders than it had the day before. "I thought you might come to see me this morning, and when you did not, I went to Leah's tent. Both of you were already gone."

"It was too hot to sleep," Rana told her. At least that much was true. "I thought to walk and get some air."

"Ah, if only there was some air!" Keziah waved her free hand in front of her face. "This time of day, there is at least a little shade outside the doorway of our tent. Come." She wound an arm through Rana's. "We can gossip and wait for Gideon to arrive back from the encampment."

Rana wanted nothing more than to go along with her. To pretend she hadn't spent the morning carrying out Asim's orders. Yet she did not move. There between the potters' tents and a tent where an old man with a long gray beard sat in the doorway with his eyes closed and his face turned up to the heavens, she saw movement in the shadows. Her body numb, her mind spinning over the regret and shame that filled her, she knew what that shadow meant. It was large. Dark. Bulky. She did not need Asim to step into the sunlight to know his eyes were on her.

He did not speak. He did not need to. His look told her she'd done her traitor's work well and efficiently that morning. It reminded her of the consequences if she dared to ask for help.

With her heart in her throat, Rana pulled away from Keziah. "I will be along in a little while," she said. "I have some things I must do."

Keziah laughed. "What is there to do in a place as desolate as this?" she asked.

Rana had always been good at lying. Yet even she couldn't come up with the words.

She didn't need to. The gray-bearded old man's eyes popped open, and he spoke, his voice as grating as a cricket's call. "Would to God we had died by the hand of the Lord in the land of Egypt," he cried out for all to hear. "Then, we sat by the fleshpots, and we ate bread to the full. Now You, our God, have brought us forth into this wilderness to kill this whole assembly with hunger."

Around them, people stopped and listened. Some murmured their agreement. Others nodded. And there at the edge of the crowd where Asim melted away as quickly and as quietly as he had materialized, Rana saw him smile with satisfaction. His plan to return the Hebrews to Egypt was working. Yes, that hyena smile told her that. It also told her something else—he had not compelled her to help him because he had to. He and the thin man and the lame fellow could do their foul work on their own. Asim had trapped Rana because he could, because he wanted her to know that he, Asim the Medjay, had the power of life and death over her. Over her dear ones.

"The poor man," Keziah said, and Rana winced before realizing it could not have been Asim who Keziah spoke of, but the old man near the tent. "He has sat too long in the sun. Otherwise, he would not be questioning our freedom or what our God expects from us."

"Do you think so?" a man nearby asked her. "It sounds to me as if, finally, someone here is speaking some sense. In Egypt, I toiled building the pharaoh's palaces and the temples to the Egyptian gods. Yes, it was backbreaking work, sunup to sunset. Yet when I was finished each day, I sat in the shade, and was given bread to eat. And sometimes beer to drink. I always had water."

"Yes." Another man joined in. "The Nile always provided us with water."

"Not when it turned to blood," a woman nearby reminded them. "What, then, did you have to drink when that happened?"

"It was Moses who turned the water at God's bidding," the man replied, and others in the crowd muttered their agreement. "It was our own God who made us thirsty, even amid the plenty that was Egypt."

"The same God who keeps us thirsty now," another man called out.

"And hungry," a woman added. "My children cry in the night. Their bellies ache with hunger."

"You see?" Rana recognized the voice that came from the back of the crowd and her stomach knotted. She turned just as the thin man who was Asim's companion strolled forward so that he could be seen by all. "You see what is happening to all of us? We listened to Moses, and Moses, he claims he listened to the Lord our God. But how do we know that is true? You remember, don't you, that Moses was raised in Pharaoh's court? He is an Egyptian. No, not by birth. But at heart. Who is to say he is not doing the bidding of his Egyptian masters, that he has not led us all out here to the middle of nowhere just as they asked him to, just so we all die?"

"That is not what our God promised!" Keziah insisted. "Moses will lead us to the land of milk and honey. That is what God promised. And we must be faithful and steadfast in our belief in Him."

"Yet if that is true, if our God proclaims we must be out here in the wilderness, if Moses says it is true, and if we believe Moses…"

The thin man looked all around, daring anyone to dispute him, and when no one did, he went right on. "Remember the taste of quail? Yes, yes, I know." He waved a hand to silence anyone who might speak. "We did not have it often. But still, we had it, eh? Now and again, we feasted on quail. And we always had bread. And water. Can you even imagine it now, the feel of cool water on your lips? The sensation of a full stomach?"

"What I remember is being beaten by my master," a man called out.

"What I remember is my husband toiling in the copper mines and meeting his death there," a woman said.

"What I remember..." The thin man looked left and right. He turned to glance at the people behind him. "What I remember was never having to worry that I would die in the middle of nowhere with my stomach empty and my mouth as dry as the sand."

Some of the people nodded. Others called out in agreement.

There was nothing more Rana wanted than to shove the thin man aside, to yell the truth so that all would hear her. *Do not listen to this man! He is a conspirator! He is one of the people causing our problems!* Yet she thought of Leah and could not, and the realization made her sick.

Keziah stood there at her side, firm in her faith despite her youth. "We will have plenty in Canaan," she told them all. "Is that not what our God tells us? If we continue to believe in Him—"

"It is impossible for dead men to believe anything," the thin man reminded them all. "How many days have we been on the road? Our provisions are nearly gone."

"That is because all do not share," someone reminded him. "Some are taking more of their share of our water. That explains why so much is missing."

The thin man looked in Rana's direction. He ran a tongue over his lips, and his eyes glinted. "Have we captured this thief? Have we ended this person's life as is our right? Day after day, we lose supplies until there is little left. Think about it. The longer we wait to decide to return to Egypt, the less food we'll have. The more we stall, the more water we will use up. What if we wait too long, eh? What if we finally see reason, and we finally decide to go back where we came from and by the time we do, what if we don't have enough provisions to get all the way back to Egypt?"

A buzz like the sound of a thousand bees went through the crowd, and people moaned.

"It is too late."

"We are already doomed."

"There is nothing we can do."

The thin man calmed them, shushing them, gesturing with his hands the way a mother might do to a child, his arms out, his hands flat, gently soothing them. "We must not lose hope. If we send a rider to Egypt now, he will arrive long before the rest of us can, and he will let the Egyptians know we are on our way. They will come out to meet us. Surely, they will. They will welcome us back with open arms."

"Welcome us back to slavery," a man growled.

"Welcome us back to full stomachs," another countered, stepping up to him.

Their argument would not end well, Rana could tell, and she backed away, prepared to melt into the shadows and be on her way.

"You are leaving?" Keziah followed her. "Don't you want to come along with me so that we might talk?"

"I will be along soon enough," Rana assured her.

Keziah pouted. "That is what you said yesterday. And the day before."

"I have been busy," Rana told her.

Keziah wrinkled her nose. "Too busy to spend time with a friend?"

"Yes." Rana scuffed her sandals in the dust. Knowing how she was endangering all the people, she could not meet Keziah's eyes. "Too busy for that."

Keziah could not possibly comprehend what she meant by this, and as always, she sloughed off the very thought and went on to the next one. "Whatever you have been doing, your skin must be terribly dry by now." She grabbed Rana's hand, nodded, and frowned. "You see, I am right. It has been days since I have applied my ointment to your hands, and your skin feels as dry as the very ground itself. You have certainly not been working with Leah's wool, or there would be some trace of sheep's lanolin on your skin. You need to come with me and—"

"No." Rana could not look Keziah in the eye when she lied, so she kept her gaze on the ground. "I do not wish to come with you."

Keziah laughed. "What are you saying? Of course you do! There is a little water in my tent, and we can share it. And can you believe it? I baked bread yesterday. I ground the grain myself too, just as a good wife would do because I thought I should have the practice in case someday I meet a man who I think is good enough for me. It is not the best-tasting bread, I admit that much. But it is edible, and

Gideon stayed at the camp last night so he has not tried any yet, but I think he'll be proud of my efforts. Since I was the only one eating it, there is plenty left. We will have a feast, and talk, and exchange news, and we will put some ointment on your hands and—"

Rana pulled her hand from Keziah's. "I said no. I do not wish to come with you."

She might have known Keziah would not give up so easily. "Gideon will be back later today," she said, a note of teasing in her voice. "I will tell you this, Sister, he has not said it in so many words, but I know my brother well enough to know what he is thinking. The last time I saw him, he asked about you. He is confused, you see. You said you would stop into our tent to dress his wound, and you have not come around. He wondered where you have been and what you have been doing. He would never admit it, of course, he tries so hard to be the strong and unemotional soldier, but I know him well enough to know he is anxious to see you again."

"Except I..." Rana moved back a step. "I am not so anxious to see him."

Keziah laughed. "Do not be silly! Of course you are! I know you well enough to see how you feel about him. But do not make a mistake, Rana, and try and play the kinds of games my mistress back in Egypt sometimes did. Games with men, I mean. Sometimes she'd greet them with wine and kisses. Other times when the mood struck her, she would pretend to be indifferent. She sometimes pretended to be aloof, don't you see, because she thought it made her more mysterious and that would make the men desire her more, when really, all it ever did was—"

"Do you ever stop talking?" Rana's words were sharp, and they cut deep, just as she meant them to. Keziah's mouth dropped open. Her eyes filled with tears. Rana pretended the very sight did not rip into her heart. "Not all of us care about trifles like husbands and bread baking and sitting for hours on end gossiping idly with a girl who knows so little about the world, she never has anything interesting to say about it," she snapped. "And as far as your brother is concerned, I do not want to see him. How much clearer can I be? He has been kind to me a time or two." She could not stop to think about it or her feigned coldness would melt in the midday sun. "But his kindness means nothing to me. Do you think I would make a good wife? Do you? And even if I was, do you think I would choose a man such as your brother?" She lifted her chin and looked Keziah in the eyes. "I am not the fool you are, Keziah. I want nothing more from you or your brother than to be left alone."

This time, she was clear enough for Keziah to understand.

That would explain why Keziah began sobbing and why, turning on her heels, she ran away.

CHAPTER SIXTEEN

That night instead of going to Leah's tent, Rana found a pocket of sand on a rocky hillside and settled there. Better the sight of the endless night sky than the bewilderment and sadness she felt when she looked at Leah's spindle sitting unused, her wool combs untouched, the blanket where she slept, empty.

She stole a morsel of bread for her evening meal, and though she told herself not to, she was so thirsty, she could not resist; when she took a waterskin from outside a tent where a blind man slept with his wife, she filled a cup for herself. The first sip was blissful. The second taste was so tainted by her misdeeds, it was more bitter even than the water of Marah, and she spit it out then poured the rest of the cup onto the ground. When it was done soaking into the earth, she kicked sand over the spot as if that alone could erase all trace of her treachery.

Before the sun rose the next morning, she was back at her task, moving through the shadows from tent to tent. If four waterskins a day was enough to make Asim happy, maybe five or six or seven would change his heart so that he took pity on Leah and set her free.

Yet it seemed there was no room for pity in Asim's heart. Not even six waterskins satisfied him that day. Discouraged, Rana returned to the rocky place where she had spent the night, far from the people whose trust she'd betrayed.

By the time she did, Keziah and Gideon were there waiting there for her.

There was no use pretending she didn't see them. There was no use running either. She knew they would follow. Instead, she hid her shame and her anger behind indifference and forced herself to join them.

Keziah twined her fingers and held her hands at her waist, and there were tears on her cheeks. Gideon, though, met her eyes.

"We know something is wrong," he said.

It was one thing being cruel to Keziah. It wasn't difficult. Keziah was innocent and sensitive. It was too easy to wound her heart.

Lying to Gideon, though, was much harder, and before she could even try, she steadied her shoulders. "Yes, something is wrong. I have come to realize I do not belong with you people. In fact, I hate it here. I wish to return to Egypt."

Keziah sniffled, and when she made to speak, Gideon put out a hand to stop her.

"There is talk in the camp," he said. "Like you, some of the others are dissatisfied. They are planning to go back to Egypt and hand themselves over again to the overseers and the slavedrivers. You are welcome to go with them. There is no one to stop you."

His words were cold and casual, a knife to her heart, and before she could betray herself and let him know how much they upset her, she turned on her heels. "Then that is exactly what I will do. I will join those people. And I will leave when they leave. And I will be happy to be done with all of you."

"Just as you are done with Leah?"

Gideon's words made Rana's insides jump and her heart squeeze, but she did not have a chance to respond before he added, "You no longer stay in her tent."

"You watch me?"

"I wonder what is happening. Leah has not been seen."

"And you cannot—" It was on the tip of her tongue to tell him he could not search for Leah, that he could not take that chance with Leah's safety. She bit back what would only cause him to ask more questions, and turned away. She called over her shoulder as she trudged in the direction of the camp. "I am not Leah's keeper."

She might have gotten all the way to where the first tents were set up if Gideon hadn't come up behind her and caught her arm. He pulled her to a stop, spun her to face him.

"We want to help you," he said, his words bitten off from between his clenched teeth.

She lifted her chin. "I do not need any help."

A muscle bunched at the base of his jaw. "I want to help you."

"Do you?" She challenged him with a look. "Is that why you said I can go back to Egypt with those who wish to return?"

He dropped her arm, turned away, whirled again, and pushed a hand through his hair. "You said you hated it here and you want to go back. I told you to go ahead, return with those fools who wish to make their way back to Egypt, and now you say—"

"You told me no one would stop me. You do not care, do you?"

"It is not my place to care if you go or stay."

That was what hurt. More than the fact that he was not troubled by the thought of her leaving.

Gideon had come right out and said it. He didn't care.

Rana bit back a sob, but before she could pepper him with lies about how she would not miss him and how she cared no more than he did, he grasped her hand in his.

"It is my place to ask what is wrong," he said.

"Why do you care? What, are we friends?"

He pulled in a long breath and let it out slowly. "You are a friend of my sister."

"But not a friend to you."

"No. You are—" Whatever he was going to say, he swallowed the words, squared his shoulders. "We want you to know that we are here for you. That is why we searched for you today. We needed to tell you. We will do whatever we can to help you."

"I do not need help from you or from anyone else. I have spent all my life helping myself."

"Yes, you have. But that was before you happened upon us, before we showed you—I hope we showed you—the value of friendship and family. That is what we are here for." He slipped his hand up to her arm, and his touch was gentle. His fingers were warm against her skin. "If you are worried, I will help alleviate your fears. If you are ill, I will find a physician who will provide the cure. If you are in trouble, Rana, know that I will move mountains to help you out of it."

She could feel the tears in her eyes, and she hated herself for it, but she did not even try to wipe them away. Her guilt choked her. Her misery trembled in her words. "What if the trouble is something even you cannot fix?"

He was arrogant enough to smile.

It was maddening.

It was endearing.

It broke her heart.

It cracked further still when Gideon lowered his voice and leaned nearer to whisper in her ear. "If you think there is such a thing as a problem I am afraid to face and cannot fix, you do not know me nearly well enough, and that in itself is a problem I must fix."

She swallowed hard. She didn't dare tell him the truth, yet she could not resist the shimmer of concern in his dark eyes. "And what would you do then, if I am the one who has caused the problem?"

"What could it possibly be?" Working through the puzzle, he backed away, cocked his head, looked her up and down. "Keziah has taught you to bake bread! That would certainly be a problem because I have eaten her bread and do not tell her this, but it is difficult to get down. I would hate to see her teach you to cook."

"It is not funny."

"No, Keziah's bread-making skills are not funny at all."

She latched onto his arm. "This is far more serious, Gideon. If you knew the truth, you would not try to make me laugh. You would hate me."

He covered her hand with his. "I think that would be impossible, Rana." He looked her in the eyes. "All I ask is that you trust me."

She didn't dare tell him the truth, yet she wanted to. More than anything. But even as the words formed on her tongue, Rana looked over Gideon's shoulder and saw Asim standing nearby. He had a knife in his hands.

Trust was a luxury. And too high a price to pay for the lives of her loved ones.

Rana yanked her hand away from Gideon's grasp.

"I no more wish to trust you than I do to talk to you," she told him, and though her stomach was knotted, her head was high when she turned and walked away from him.

As the days went by, the people got more and more worried about their water supplies, and Rana no longer dared to go out during the daylight to do Asim's bidding. She hid among the shepherds' tents and waited until after the sun went down before she prowled the camp again, and all the time she did, one thought burned in Rana's head. Like Set, she was the instrument of chaos. In order for her to assure Leah's safety, she must cause others to suffer, and the very thought made her choke with anger, and despair filled her. All this time, and she still had no idea where Leah was. After all this time, Leah must think she'd been forgotten, abandoned.

All this time.

That day she stood outside his tent, what had the old man said about the Hebrew God? That He had brought them into the wilderness to kill the whole assembly with hunger?

"Then so be it," Rana grumbled, leaning low to take hold of a waterskin that had been left outside the tent of a widow. "If that is so, I am an instrument of their God, and their God…" She blinked back tears, stood up, and searched the heavens. Could the Hebrew God hear her? Did He read the thoughts that burned through her brain? "Their God will understand," she said. "If He sees into my heart, He will understand. All I do, I do to keep Leah alive." But even that did not console her.

She stowed that waterskin in the shadow of some scrubby bushes outside of camp and went back for another, this time to where the stonecutters had their tents. The last of their fires sputtered, and there was no one around. She kept herself to the shadows, searching for more waterskins, and catching sight of a familiar shape nearby, Rana smiled.

She skirted a fire, closed in on a skin, and slung it over her shoulder.

"No! Do not! Rana, do not!"

Recognizing Keziah's voice, Rana spun around.

"What are you doing?" Tears streamed over Keziah's cheeks, and her voice was sharp and shrill. In the nighttime silence of the camp, it was loud enough to attract a crowd, and it did. One by one, the stonecutters and their families stepped out of their tents and into the halos of firelight. One by one, brickmakers got up from their meager meals and joined them. One by one, person by person, they closed in on Rana and Keziah, and Rana let the waterskin slip to her side.

She had no time to explain, so she didn't even try. She sent a look to Keziah that told her to run while she could. Keziah didn't get the message. Or she didn't care. Or perhaps she was too blinded by her tears to see.

A short, burly man with a heavy beard was the first to come closer. "What is happening here?" he demanded. "What are you doing near our tents? And you!" When he looked at Rana, his eyes glinted like metal in a forge. "Why did you have one of our waterskins?"

"She is not doing anything," Keziah insisted. "We are dear friends, and we were simply out walking and—"

"We were not out walking," Rana told the man, because she could see what Keziah was trying to do and she couldn't bear the thought of Keziah being accused along with her. "I was here alone. I have no idea why Keziah is here."

"Because I have been looking for you," Keziah said out of the side of her mouth. "And then I finally caught sight of you, and so I followed you, and—" She sniffled and tears glistened on her cheeks like jewels. "The darkness must be playing tricks on my eyes. I cannot have seen what I thought I saw. Rana, you would not—" She remembered the people crowded around them and knew better than to say more. She snatched up Rana's hands. "Do not say another word. You can explain it all later. For now, come with me. Quickly. I will take you to the camp where Gideon is tonight."

"You will not." The man with the hard gaze stepped into their path and behind him, the crowd of men and women stepped forward. It did not take a lifetime of being a thief to recognize the danger. A wall of people in front of them, a row of tents behind them. Rana knew their escape routes were blocked. If she was alone, she would have attempted to knock down the man who challenged her. If she was back in Pithom, she would have tossed an accusation at the closest person at hand as a diversion. But she was with Keziah. And Keziah was innocent of any wrong. She didn't dare risk anyone thinking they were co-conspirators.

"You there." The man poked his chin forward at Rana. "You were not walking. You had a waterskin, one that we can all see clearly on the ground next to you now. Explain yourself."

"She was probably trying to protect your water supply." Keziah stepped forward. "That is the kind of person Rana is. It seems to me, Shimon the stonecutter, you should thank Rana, not accuse her. I do not see any of you patrolling the camp, looking for those who steal our water. Yet that is obviously what she is doing. Does this young woman have more courage than you, Shimon?" She looked from man to man. "Does she have more courage than any of you?"

They shuffled their feet in the dust and looked away, and the tension that had built in Rana's chest eased.

"We must offer a prayer of thanksgiving," Keziah said, her voice ringing with a certainty Rana had never heard in it before. "Here and now. We should be grateful God has given us those who care more for the welfare of our people than they do for themselves."

"No." Rana could not take the pain of listening to her. "They should not be grateful. They should—"

"Oh, God, our Father and our Protector." Keziah raised her voice and started into her prayer as if Rana had not spoken. "We humbly ask You to hear us and give Your blessings to those like this woman"—she drew Rana nearer—"who care for Your people."

"Care? This woman does not care for us!" A woman's shrill voice split the night. Her eyes ablaze, her voice shaking, she came from the area where last Rana had done her traitor's work and joined the crowd. "I have just taken a count of our skins. One of them is missing."

"Well, then..." Shimon darted forward. "It seems to me we have found the thief who takes our water and leaves us parched."

"I have seen her in the camp before," a woman called out. "They say she is an Egyptian."

"And the Egyptians," another woman hissed, "are angry that we are free. They want us to die here in the wilderness."

"That is not what you said yesterday." Her fists on her hips, Keziah cast a look all around. "Yesterday, you stood very near here and listened to the man who told you that if we went back to Egypt, our former masters would welcome us with open arms. You were willing to think the best of the Egyptians then."

"And we will be more likely to go back, back into slavery, if there is no water to drink." Another man stepped closer, two more behind him.

"Seize her and tie her up!" someone yelled, and seeing the anger in their eyes, Rana's heart jumped into her throat when as one, the people moved toward her. Before they could get any closer, though, Keziah cried out, "Stop. Do not let your emotions get in the way of your reason. At least let us listen to what Rana has to say. I am sure she has an explanation."

"I want no explanation," a man called out. "I want water! And food!"

"And I want her punished," a brickmaker shouted. "Our infants and our old people are weak with thirst and hunger. If this is the person responsible—"

"If this is the person responsible," Keziah's voice trembled, yet she carried on, "then we will deal with it in a way that is right and just. One of you, go to the camp and call my brother here. I am sure you will agree, Gideon is a fair and honest man. We will let him hear what Rana has to say, and then, if he sees fit, he will take Rana to Moses."

"Why wait so long?" A man at the edge of the crowd bent and retrieved a rock and hurled it. It struck Rana on the shoulder and she winced and cried out. A second man threw another stone, and this one had a rough edge. It hit her arm and drew blood.

"We must wait!" Keziah screamed. "You are forgetting that Rana has traveled with us all the way from Pithom. And in that time, she has been a good friend to many of you. She has pulled carts along with you and she has gathered wool."

"Yes, but now she has betrayed us," a man said. "And there is only one punishment for such disloyalty. She must be stoned!"

Keziah folded Rana into her arms and held her close.

"No! You will be hurt!" Rana screamed just as the first stones flew at her. One hit her ear. Another slammed into her leg. There was only one thing she could do, and she knew she had to act quickly. She grabbed hold of Keziah and shoved her as hard as she could, and she crashed into the crowd. Shimon was knocked off his feet, and when he went down, he bumped into a woman who landed on top of him. A roar of anger went up from the crowd, and while they were still trying to sort themselves out, Rana darted away.

She stopped for one second only to look back and mouth the words "I am sorry" to Keziah, then she took off into the night and melted into the shadows.

CHAPTER SEVENTEEN

Word would travel the camp like lightning.

The thought hammered through Rana even as her feet pounded the dry earth.

The stonemasons and brickmakers who were so quick to accuse her and so eager to punish her would shout the news to the wheelwrights whose tents were pitched nearby. The wheelwrights would spread the story to the spinners and the dyers, and because the spinners and the dyers worked so closely with the shepherds, the shepherds, too, would know the details even before Rana was far enough away from the glow of the pillar of fire at the center of the camp to dare to stop and take a breath.

The shepherds would tell the farmworkers, and they would inform the women who stood outside their tents in the hopes of catching the touch of a cool night breeze.

And once the women knew...

Rana's stomach twisted and soured. Each breath she gulped in of the hot night air burned her lungs.

Hebrew women were not so unlike Egyptian women, and like Egyptian women, they loved to gossip. What better story to tell than this?

The traitor had been discovered!

What would happen to Leah when Asim heard?

The thought hit her like a punch, and she sobbed. He would be angry that Rana had been so careless as to be caught and so he'd lost his accomplice. Yet perhaps he would rejoice at the same time. Rana had run off into the wilderness. Alone.

Back in Pithom, Asim had sworn he would kill her. Now, he would have his ultimate revenge. Without food and water, without the support of the people she'd come to rely on, she would surely die.

"So be it." Her voice wavered over the words, and whatever energy she had found in the excitement of fleeing the Hebrews drained away completely. "Perhaps he will take my death in exchange for Leah's freedom."

There in a spot where there was little to shelter her, and nothing to eat, and no sounds to disturb the night except for the shrill cries of hyenas in the distance, she stopped running. Her knees gave way, and she slumped onto the dry ground and raised her eyes to the heavens.

"All that I ask, God of the Hebrews," she prayed, "is that Leah does not suffer because of what I have done. That the people do not think Keziah was there to help me and, so, punish her. And please make it so that in days to come when they think of me, when Gideon remembers me..." Tears clouded her vision and choked her words, and she bowed her head. "After I am dead, make it so that when he remembers me, it is not as a traitor but for whatever little good was in me. The time I dressed the wound on his arm. The times we shared a smile. Even the time he caught me with the donkey." Despite herself, she laughed. "Make it so that he remembers the donkey, and he smiles too, and tell him not to think badly of me because I did not listen to him. If I trusted him like he asked me to…"

Trust.

The word reverberated through her mind like thunder. It shivered in her soul, and it was there, deep within her being, that for the first time, she understood.

The Hebrew people trusted God and obeyed His commands. Even through hundreds of years of slavery, they held onto that trust, and in doing so, they showed their faith. Back in Pithom, Rana would not have believed it was possible, but she had seen proof of it time and again as she traveled with them. They trusted Him, and He brought plagues down on Egypt and led His people out of bondage. They trusted Him, and He changed bitter water to sweet. They trusted him, and He showed them the way to wells of fresh water. He was with them day and night, cloud and fire, guiding them not just to freedom but to a land that would be their own, the land He promised them that would be filled with milk and honey.

Now their faith was being tested again. They were thirsty, and they were on the brink of starvation. Trust had sustained their people for many hundreds of years, and now many had lost that trust.

And Rana was one of them.

Her tears flowed, and though she told herself it would break her heart, she looked over her shoulder in the direction of the camp. Somewhere back there in the darkness were the people she'd come to love. Yet because she feared for Leah, she hadn't dared to tell Gideon about the saboteurs in the camp. She hadn't trusted Keziah enough to share her worries.

"And what if even though I am gone from the camp, it does not make a difference?"

The realization shot through Rana like a thunderbolt, and she sprang to her feet.

Leah might still be in danger, and so would the Hebrew people. Asim and his men would continue to steal and hide their supplies. With little food and little water, God's people were doomed.

All because Rana didn't trust herself or her love enough to ask for help. Because she didn't trust God.

"They will not be happy to see you again," she told herself even as she dusted off her tunic and turned back to the camp. "They will surely drag you before Moses and Aaron, and a rightful punishment will be given to you. The last thing you see upon this earth will be the sorrow in Keziah's eyes. The last thing you feel will be the anguish that flows from Gideon like a wave. For all you have done, you will be stoned to death."

Even that thought did not stop her. She raced toward the camp.

It was time for her to put her faith in her dear ones. It was time for her to trust God to lead her.

With her footsteps fueled by her determination, Rana was halfway back to the camp when a flash of bright light caught her eye.

She stopped and looked up and to her left just in time to see a meteor streak the sky, its tail like glittering silver, the arc of its path leading over distant hills.

And that is when she saw something else.

A glimmer, no more. A trail of light that snaked along the side of a hill, following a crooked path.

As if someone with an oil lamp was walking there.

"Leah?" The name escaped her in a whisper of wonder. She knew it could not be the spinner walking there. But one of her captors? Who else would be so far from the camp at so dark a time? The very idea made Rana's heart clutch.

You cannot be as lucky as that, she told herself. Yet she knew this had nothing to do with luck. She raised her eyes to the sky, whispered a quick "thank You," and followed the light.

In the night, distances in the wilderness can be deceiving. Rana was not nearly as far from the light as she thought. Her eyes still trained on it, she found herself at the base of the hill in just a short time, and when the light came nearer, she pressed herself to the far side of a boulder and held her breath. In the nighttime quiet, she heard the crunch of sandals against the rocky ground, the grumble of a man's voice.

"She refuses to eat," she heard a man say. When another man responded with, "Asim will not be pleased. The old woman will be worth nothing if she is dead," she was glad she'd approached quietly and concealed herself quickly.

"She will reconsider. Eventually," the first man said, and the men's footsteps receded into the dark. "I left the bread there with her. Mark my words, it will be gone by morning."

Whatever else they said as they walked away, Rana wasn't sure. Her heart beat so fast and so hard, she could hear only the whooshing of her blood in her ears. She could feel only the relief and gratitude that washed through her like the waters of the Red Sea they'd come through unscathed.

Leah was alive, and hidden just nearby!

She'd already pushed away from the boulder and started up the hill when Rana realized it was madness to try to go farther. With no light to lead her, she could easily get lost or be injured. Her only hope—the only hope for Leah's rescue—was to get help.

Yet even if she did, how could she explain where Leah was? How would she find her way back to this place?

The question did not trouble her for long. Rana stripped off her woolen tunic, and before she donned it again, she removed the linen sheath she wore next to her skin. It had already been ripped to dress Gideon's wound. It took nothing at all to tear small pieces from the rest of the dress and drop it here and there along her path, all the way back to the camp.

When Rana arrived at the camp again, the night sky was still a black as deep as a scarab carved from obsidian. There was no one yet awake and moving.

Except for one man, silhouetted against the light of the pillar of fire.

She did not need to study the width of his shoulders or his height. She did not need to see the outline of the sword at his waist. It was not eyesight or even instinct that led her back to him. It was trust and faith. With those to guide her, she would know him anywhere.

Rana's heart pounded. Her throat knotted. She raced forward and did not care if every person in the camp heard her and knew the traitor had returned. She called out, "Gideon!" and saw him turn, and after that, she did not need to run all the way to meet him because he ran to her, and they met just where the first tents were pitched. She wanted to throw her arms around him, but the emotion that simmered in his eyes stopped her.

A momentary flash of disappointment.

A look of deep sadness.

Much confusion.

All of it brightened suddenly with astonishing relief.

"I thought I would never see you again." His voice was heavy with emotion. "Rana, I thought—"

"Yes, I know." She could not wait another moment. She threw her arms around him and his arms went around her too, and she nestled her head against his shoulder and wished the moment would last forever. If only she had the luxury!

"You were right," she told him, backing out of his arms, looking into his eyes. "I should have trusted you with the truth of what is happening, but Gideon, I was so afraid. Leah—" Her voice broke. Tears stained her cheeks. "It is Asim, the Medjay. He is here in the camp. He has taken Leah, and in exchange for her life, he demanded my help stealing waterskins. He wants them for himself so that when he returns to Egypt, he has water along the way."

Gideon's shoulders went rigid. His eyes flared with anger. "You were compelled to—" Outrage choked him, and Rana's heart squeezed.

"I did not dare tell you and have you and other soldiers search for her and so risk Leah's safety. It is why I have avoided you, Gideon. Why I have been cruel to Keziah. But now, I have found Leah!"

"You have?" It was not amusement that brightened his expression. It was wonder, and respect. It was admiration. The next second, it was all washed away with concern. "If you risked yourself to search for her—"

"I did not," she assured him. "I can only think—" She remembered the glory of the meteor flashing through the sky and the way seeing it had directed her attention to the hills, and she corrected her words. "I know I did not find her on my own. God showed me the way."

"And you trusted Him and followed where He led you. And now you trust me with this information."

"Only if you trust that I am not a traitor to the people. I did what I had to do. All for Leah. And now we must work together and save her, Gideon. If Asim finds I was anywhere near—"

"We will not let him. I have a trained band of comrades. We can be quick, and we can be quiet." He turned toward the soldier's encampment.

"And I will come with you," Rana told him. "Otherwise, how will you find Leah?"

His expression told her he hated to admit it, but it was a very good question. "How will you find her? In the wilderness. In the dark. Surely it is easy to get confused."

"Not when you leave a trail for yourself." She smiled because though the situation was grave, she was pleased by her own cunning. "Pieces of my linen sheath," she told him. "One here, one there. There is no breeze to blow them around, and if we head there"—she pointed—"toward those hills, we will surely find the cloth and it will lead our way."

"No." He took hold of her shoulders, drew her near, and planted a quick kiss on her forehead. "My comrades and I will surely find our way now that you have revealed your clever plan. You will stay here, Rana. You must. For Leah's sake."

For Leah's sake, she did, even when Gideon left for the camp, even when she saw him again in the distance, a deeper shadow in the dark that filled all the air around them, he and his men moving as quickly and as quietly as if they were no more than a dream in the night.

She waited, and while she waited, she prayed. For Leah's safety. For the welfare of the soldiers who had gone on the mission to rescue her. For Gideon.

"He is a good man," she whispered, though she was sure the God of the Hebrews, her God now, knew that full well. "And I believe I have done something I never thought I would do. I have fallen in love with him."

She did not know how long she sat there with the thought, she only knew that when she raised her head again, when she opened her eyes, the first touches of daylight dappled the far eastern horizon. It was then she saw them coming. Two soldiers. Leah walking between them then running when she caught sight of Rana.

But Gideon?

Even as Leah and Rana fell into each other's arms, even as Rana thanked God for the spinner's safety, she looked over Leah's shoulders, her vision clouded by sudden tears.

And then she saw a soldier leading the thin man bound in ropes. Another soldier urging on the man with a limp. And Gideon.

Rana's heart leaped into her throat. Asim was taller than Gideon. Broader. Yet he walked, bound and defeated, at Gideon's side.

Leah must surely have known exactly what Rana was thinking. Exactly where she was looking. "Go." She patted Rana's shoulder. "Go to him. And I..." She backed away and toward the camp. "I believe after all these days, all I would like to do is return to my tent and comb some wool."

The other two soldiers moved forward and took charge of Asim, and the four soldiers together took their prisoners to the encampment. Alone now, Gideon ran to Rana and she to him.

His left eye was blackened. There was dirt on his cheek. The bandage she had so carefully wound around his arm was soaked with blood. But when he threw his arms around Rana, she didn't care. She only knew that he was safe, and it was all that mattered.

Just at that moment, as daylight split the horizon and in the golden light, the dew that lay upon the ground around them sparked and flashed like gemstones. A moment more of sunlight and the dew dissolved, and when it did, an even more remarkable sight presented itself.

"Gideon." Rana pointed, but she didn't need to. Like Rana, he looked to where a white substance glimmered on rocks and coated the earth like the snow Rana had heard told about in stories. It was everywhere. Round, and as small as a coriander seed.

Gideon was a rational and reasonable man, and his first reaction was to stoop and touch a finger to the matter. "It is nothing I have ever seen before. Like something that comes to us through—"

"A miracle!"

CHAPTER EIGHTEEN

Rana did not hesitate. Trusting the truth that burned in her heart, she stooped, took up a handful of the substance, and tasted it.

"It tastes like wafers sweetened with honey," she told Gideon.

He sucked in a breath of surprise. "It is just as God promised." He, too, tasted the substance, smiled, and explained. "Last night, after you…" An instant of memory, of worry, darkened his expression, but it was soon overshadowed by the wonder of the moment. "After you left, Moses gathered us, and he listened to the concerns of the people. They were hungry and thirsty, and some were angry. At you. At God. Some talked about returning to Egypt. Others were less willing to find a solution to the problem and were only looking to stir up trouble. They railed against Moses and Aaron and the leaders of the twelve tribes, and they threatened revolt and violence. And Moses, though I believe he could have called upon God to bring down judgment on those who preached hate and anger, Moses simply listened. To everything everyone had to say. And when the people were done speaking, this is what he told us." Remembering it all, his eyes shimmered with emotion.

"Moses said the Lord would give us flesh to eat in the evening. And Rana, no sooner had the words left his mouth than a flock of quail overtook the camp. It was a wonder! We captured the quail and feasted on them. The old and very young were made whole again. And people gathered around the cooking fires and shared a meal and prayers and friendship. The food was delicious and..." When he looked at her, his smile was sweet and soft. "I looked for you. I even took some roasted quail with me so if I found you, you could join in the celebration. But you..." When his voice broke, she squeezed his hand. "By then, you were gone. You were alone, somewhere in the night."

"It was a good thing I did not catch scent of the feast," she told him, smiling. "Or I would have raced back to the camp no matter how angry everyone was at me! And the quail! What a sight that must have been. How good God is to us. That was His miracle, surely."

"Yes, but there is more, and until this very moment, I did not understand it. God also told Moses He would rain bread from heaven for us and that the people would go out and gather it. He said He would do it to prove to them that they walk in His law and so that..." Gideon paused, recalling the words.

"'You will know that the Lord has brought you out of the land of Egypt and in the morning, you will see the glory of the Lord, for He has heard your murmurings.'" He let out a shaky breath. "And now this! This is God's promise, the bread the Lord has given us to eat."

Rana laughed, took up more of the substance, and shared it with Gideon, and they ate, and when she finished, she licked her lips. "It is delicious."

"And from the texture of it..." He'd had quail to eat the evening before. He was not as hungry as Rana and hadn't eaten all she'd given him. He still had one perfect white seed in his hand, and he rolled it in his fingers. "I believe it can be ground and made into bread."

"Keziah's bread?" Rana asked.

Gideon laughed. "Even Keziah could not ruin the taste of something this wonderful."

"Yes, but what is it?"

"What is it?" Gideon considered this. "That is a very good question, and when you ask it, it sounds like the words *man hu*, words we use to ask what something is. So, unless Moses tells us differently, that is what we will call it! Manna. It is God's gift."

"God's sweet gift from heaven." Rana could not resist. She took another handful of manna and gulped it down. "We must wake everyone in the camp so they can see what God has done for us. We can help them collect it, and if we store it wisely, we will eat for a very long time."

"First we must tell Moses." Gideon started for the center of the camp, where Moses had his tent.

As the dew had done just minutes earlier, Rana's excitement melted away, and her stomach twisted as if there was a cold hand inside her. She held back. "I cannot go before Moses. He will have heard by now about the waterskins. He will know how I took them, and he will not know why. He will think that I am a traitor to the people."

Gideon came back to stand before her. "I asked you to trust me, and Rana, you did. You came back to the camp to ask for my help, and you see how your faith resulted in not only Leah's rescue but in this reward of manna from heaven. Now you must trust me again. You will tell Moses all, and I will not let anything happen to you."

Rana swallowed her misgivings and put her hand in his. "Yes, it is time for everyone to know the truth."

She was not surprised to see the shepherds up and about on the way to Moses's tent. They were always first to rise, and when they did and saw the manna on the ground, they made a great noise of rejoicing. Their laughs and calls woke their neighbors, and seeing the manna, tasting it, and knowing it was a gift from God, those people shouted prayers of thanksgiving.

"Food!" A woman twirled and danced in their path, her hands filled with manna, a smile on her face.

"Proof that our God is the One True God," a man said, and he tasted the manna and called his wife and his children from his tent so that they, too, could eat.

All around the camp, people sang and laughed and took up handfuls of manna to taste it, and once they had, they remarked on the goodness of it, and already, there were old women grinding it, eager to turn it into bread.

It was a happy celebration.

Until their gazes fell on Rana.

Then the people stopped collecting manna. They fell silent. Their eyes narrowed with suspicion, they stood and watched her pass, and Rana heard them grumble.

"Egyptian."

"Traitor."

"She disguised herself as one of us."

"She took our water. She wanted us to die."

Rana did not look right or left. Her chin high and her hand clasped tightly in Gideon's, she kept walking, and when a small stone flew at her and struck the back of her head, she refused to flinch or cry out. She saw Gideon's jaw tighten though. He saw who'd thrown the stone, and sooner or later, the man would come to regret his action.

By the time they made their way to Moses's tent, the people had gathered behind them, and Moses was standing outside.

"What is happening?" he asked.

"Our God has sent a gift from heaven to sustain us. The people are excited and rejoicing." Gideon scooped up manna and handed it to Moses, who took it, tasted it, and nodded.

"Our God is good to us," Moses said.

"And we will collect what is all around us here on the ground," a woman called out. "And we will fill our stomachs and eat for days."

A shout of joy welcomed her comment.

That is, until Moses said, "You will not."

Now the people grumbled.

"What are you talking about?"

"You cannot mean it. We need this food from heaven to stay alive."

"You are like this traitor." A man spat in Rana's direction. "She, too, wishes us to die out here in the wilderness."

"No one is going to die." Moses quieted the man with a look. "But this is what you must do." There was a wide, flat rock nearby, and with the help of his brother, Aaron, Moses stepped onto it, the better to be seen. "You will collect manna for yourself and for your families. Take cups and scoop it up. One omer each. That is ten cups for every man, woman, and child in your tent."

"But there is plenty," a man shouted. "Why limit how much we take? We can keep it and know that tomorrow, we will have food to eat."

"One omer per person," Moses told him.

"And then what are we to do tomorrow?" A woman's shrill voice split the morning. "And the morning after that? And the one after that? You tell us to gather and bake today. And tomorrow? Do you expect us to starve again tomorrow?"

Moses's eyes flashed. His cheeks turned a dark, ugly shade. "You dare to ask?" he bellowed. "Our God has done great and wonderful things for us, and you dare to ask about tomorrow? Were you hungry last night?" He cast a look all around, and the people nodded and mumbled their replies.

"You were hungry, and God sent you quail. You were hungry this morning, and now you have this—"

His gaze traveled automatically to Gideon, who said, "Manna."

Moses thanked him with a quick smile. "This morning, God has rained manna down on us like a blessing. And He will do it tomorrow and the next day and the next to prove His love for us. But in return, we must show our faith in Him. Our trust."

Rana squeezed Gideon's hand.

"Did you hear that?" Aaron called out. "One omer of manna a day for each person."

Moses nodded. "If you take more," he warned them, "it will be inedible by tomorrow. Every morning you must collect it fresh. And every day, you must use it. And on the sixth day from today, you will take two portions for each of the people in your tents so that on the seventh day, you can rest and not have to gather manna and bake it into bread. Do you understand the words of the Lord?"

The people said they did, so Moses continued. "Then go about your business." He shooed them away. "Collect your daily portion. And thank the Lord our God for all He has done for us."

Yet the people did not budge, and Moses looked from man to man. "What is it?" he asked.

Shimon the stonecutter stepped forward. "It is this woman. She is the one who was found stealing waterskins last night. She was doing her best to make sure we died of thirst. She ran away, but now she is back, and yes, God has sent us manna from heaven, but that does not change anything she did to hurt us. She must be punished!"

A roar of approval went up all around, and two men stepped forward to seize Rana. When Gideon's eye blazed and he put a hand to his sword, they changed their minds and fell back into the crowd.

Moses stepped down from the rock and came close enough to Rana so he did not need to raise his voice.

"Is it true what they say?" he asked her.

"Yes." Her eyes welled and she looked at the ground.

Moses put a hand to her chin and lifted it. "You stole our water?"

"Yes," she said again.

He cocked his head, considering her. "These people, they want you to pay for your transgressions with your life."

Rana swallowed hard. "Yes."

"Yet something tells me there is more to the story."

Relief swept over her. "Yes," she told Moses. "There is."

"Come then." He put a hand on her shoulder and led her toward his tent. "Come tell me all about it."

CHAPTER NINETEEN

Moses did not tell Shimon and the others they could not follow, and they took that as an invitation to gather outside Moses's tent even when he held back the flap over the doorway and motioned Rana inside.

She hesitated and looked back over her shoulder at the crowd.

"No," she told Moses. "If you will allow it, I would speak in front of all the people. They need to know the truth of what happened."

She saw Moses and Gideon exchange looks. But neither man questioned her decision. Moses kept his place. Gideon stayed at Rana's side when she stepped forward, her fingers twined at her waist, her shoulders squared.

"You all heard what I said to Moses," she told them, her voice loud and as clear as the endless morning sky. "I admitted to him, and I admit to all of you, I have taken your waterskins."

"You are a traitor!" Shimon the stonecutter called out.

"And when we are dead," a woman yelled, "you will be a murderer too."

"And murderers pay for their sin with their lives," another screamed.

Gideon slapped a hand to his sword, and Rana knew that in another second, he would march into the crowd and quiet the protesters in his own fashion. She did not give him the chance but reached for his hand and held on tightly. There was strength in his touch, comfort in the feel of his steady pulse against hers.

"You need to know my reasons for what I did," she told the people. "You see, it started because there are spies here within the camp."

Shimon was so overcome with emotion, he jumped up and down. "She admits it. She says she is a spy."

"I did not say I was one of them," Rana pointed out. "And truly, I did not wish to hurt anyone." She turned to Moses, and encouraged by the kindness in his dark eyes, she added for his ears alone, "You know I am an Egyptian, and the spies I speak of, they, too, are Egyptians."

Moses pursed his lips, considering this. "If this is true, surely we would have noticed them by now."

"No one has noticed me particularly," she reminded him. "I am dressed as you dress. So are these men who wish you harm. I eat the foods you eat. So do they. And though I did not know your prayers or your God when we started out from Pithom, I have learned all that now."

"And you believe as we believe?"

To Rana, this seemed far more important even than the question of her guilt. Yet she did not stop to consider it. She didn't have to. The truth of the matter fired her blood and settled in her heart and there, it filled a lifetime of emptiness.

"Yes." Rana bowed her head to acknowledge the truth of her testimony before she raised her voice and turned back to the crowd. "Just as you have, I have seen God's wonders and His miracles. Just as you do, I seek to follow His word and do His bidding in all things. This morning, I saw manna appear out of the heavens, just as all of you did. I know the goodness of God. I trust that He will care for us and lead us to Canaan."

"What does trust have to do with you wanting us to die here of thirst?" someone demanded.

"A valid question." Rana shook her head to clear it, to make sure she could line up the words she wanted to say so that the people heard, so that they understood. "I betrayed your trust, just as I betrayed all of you. I freely admit as much." Keziah and Leah stepped to the front of the crowd, and seeing them, Rana's eyes filled with tears, but she forced herself to look away from them. If she thought about how Keziah had become the sister she never had, if she stopped to consider what might have happened to Leah, and how she'd turned her back on both of them rather than trust them with the truth, she would never be able to continue.

"Now," she said, "I must learn to trust you all. I must trust that if I tell you what happened, you will understand and that you will find it in your hearts to think kindly of me."

Moses's beard twitched. "You are putting yourself at risk, you know. These people..." He did not need to sweep an arm out toward the crowd. Rana could hear their mumblings, and she knew it wouldn't be long before they could not control their anger. They would not dare cast stones at her, not with Moses nearby. Not with Gideon on hand to defend her. But there were many in the crowd, and it would not be so difficult for them to rise up, to seize her and drag her away.

Moses leaned close and spoke in her ear. "They are not in a forgiving mood."

She was certain of it, and her heart ached at the thought. "The Lord understands," she replied. "And if our God knows the truth of the matter and forgives, then perhaps His people will as well."

When Shimon shifted from foot to foot, the grit beneath his feet sounded like breaking bones. "You say these things about spies, but why should we believe you?"

"You, too, must trust." Leah stepped forward. "Believe me when I tell you there are saboteurs here in the camp, Egyptians who have been sent by Pharaoh to convince us to return to Egypt. I know this because for the last days, I have been their prisoner."

A buzz went through the crowd, but Rana silenced them. "They want you back, you see. The Egyptians. It did not take long after our exodus for them to realize that without the slaves that keep the wheels of the empire turning, there is no empire at all. They knew if we were hungry enough, if we were thirsty enough—"

"It is just as that man told us," Leah said, stepping forward and facing the crowd. "In Marah. The man who urged us to gather together and return to Egypt. He was one of those who accosted me one morning when I was out collecting wool, one of the men who held me in a cave in the far hills. You listened to him, many of you. And he nearly stole the hope that feeds our hearts and fuels our footsteps."

Shimon was not convinced. "That man spoke sense. And you're telling us he is one of these…what did you call them? Saboteurs?"

For the first time, Rana spoke to Shimon directly. "Did you recognize that man?" she asked him. "Had you ever seen him when you lived in Goshen?"

Shimon's nose twitched. "There are many here in the camp. We cannot know them all."

"Did any of you?" Rana looked around the crowd. "Some of you were willing to follow him back to Egypt. Yet did any of you even know the man's name?"

When no one answered, she went on. "He is one of them. He, and another man, one with a twisted leg. And"—even speaking his name made Rana feel as if she was choking—"they are under the command of an Egyptian named Asim."

"The Medjay?" A woman's voice trembled with fear. "We knew him well enough in Goshen. He and his rod and the Medjay he brought with him when he stalked our streets looking for even the smallest offense so he could punish us."

"Such a terrible man, and yet, you admit to being in league with him." Shimon's eyes were dark and small, like a ferret's, and they glittered with resentment.

"I admit only to being naive and afraid," Rana said. "If I had told all from the start…" She looked at Gideon. "I knew Leah was being held against her will, and I was compelled to help steal waterskins in exchange for her life."

"Instead of wishing to punish her," Gideon said, stepping forward, "we should be thanking Rana for all she's done. Even now, soldiers are in the hills retrieving the waterskins that were hidden there."

"Just like that?" Shimon wasn't convinced. His voice was high with disbelief. "You believe this woman just like that? What proof has she shown us? She tells us a story about spies and Medjay and the way she talks about these men, she makes them sound powerful and invincible like the pagan demons she and the other Egyptians believe in. And yet you, Gideon, a man of your courage and your reputation, you believe her?"

"I believed her from the start," Gideon said. "But if you need proof…" He motioned to a soldier stationed nearby and he, in turn, waved toward his comrades. The next minute, a phalanx of soldiers marched into the area leading Asim and his men.

"Here are the real traitors," Gideon said. "And here"—he put a hand on Rana's shoulder— "is the woman who made it possible for us to capture them and save Leah's life."

They waited until it was nearly nightfall, because although Asim and his co-conspirators were not worthy of such kindness, Moses said that all people deserve as much from those who believe in an almighty God. Supplies were packed for them, waterskins loaded. Three donkeys were readied, and though Rana told herself it was foolish, she was glad the donkey she stole so long before was not one of them. She hated to think her donkey would live out its days with Asim.

The people gathered and watched the preparations, and when all was ready, Moses and Aaron and the leaders of the twelve tribes stepped forward, and Moses instructed the men to mount their donkeys. "Egypt is west," he said, pointing toward the setting sun. "And we are going east. There is no reason we should ever see any of you again."

The lame man needed help to mount his donkey.

The thin man sniveled and moaned, and once he was up on the donkey, his shoulders drooped and he wept.

Asim snarled and cursed, but he did not fight against the people who surrounded him. Even he knew mercy when he saw it.

"West to Egypt." Moses stood at Rana's side, and he leaned closer to her. "It will be a long and difficult journey, but they are healthy men, they will reach their goal. We have prepared a fourth donkey with extra supplies. If you wish it, you can leave with them."

"The only thing I wanted for a very long time was to go back," she told him. "And now..." She looked to where Gideon and the other soldiers stood at attention on either side of the path the three men would take out of the camp. Like grim statues, their features were set, their hands on swords and bows. If Asim and the others dared to defy the order of Moses and the will of the people, they would pay the ultimate price.

Watching Gideon, seeing his strength and his determination, her heart fluttered. Her soul flooded with peace. Rana smiled. "Now this my home."

Leah was nearby, and she let go a long sigh that trailed into the night sky.

Keziah sniffled, but Rana knew her tears were ones of joy.

They watched the men start off until they disappeared into the gathering night. It was then that Moses put a hand on Rana's shoulder.

"There are matters we need to discuss," he said.

"Yes." She had expected as much, and when he turned toward his tent along with Aaron, she followed, and once they were inside, she kept her place at the doorway and glanced around. The tent of Moses was not much bigger than the one Keziah and Gideon shared, and no more extravagant. A few carpets thrown on the ground. Three cushions around a table. Moses and Aaron sat on two of them, but even when Moses waved her to join them, Rana kept her place.

Her stomach was cold, but her faith never faltered. "I know I deserve to be punished for what I have done," she told them.

There was bread on a plate on the table, and Moses reached for a piece, tore it in two, and offered half to Rana. She was too nervous to eat, too aware of the hospitality being offered not to. She accepted the bread, took a bite, and grinned. The bread had surely been made from ground manna, for nothing else could taste as wonderful.

It wasn't until she had eaten and Moses had finished his bread that he spoke.

"Four hundred years ago," he said, "our ancestor, Joseph, was sold into slavery in Egypt. You know the story?"

Rana shook her head.

"Joseph was his father's favorite," Moses explained, "and his half brothers were jealous. They wanted rid of him. They talked about killing him, but instead, they sold him. But Joseph was very wise, and he had the gift of interpreting dreams. He went to Egypt as a slave, and he became a trusted advisor to the pharaoh, and eventually, vizier, second only to Pharaoh in power and praise."

"In Egypt, we were never told the story," Rana said. "There was no talk of so important a Hebrew."

"Well, there should have been," Aaron grumbled, but Moses silenced him with a small movement of his hand.

"There was a famine, one that lasted seven years, and in that time, Joseph saved the people of Egypt. He had predicted the famine, you see, and he made sure there were stores of grain so that the people had the food they needed. The famine was widespread. It even affected Joseph's family in Canaan, and they went to Egypt to escape it and were given the land of Goshen to settle in."

"And they later became slaves," Rana said.

Moses nodded. "It is true, but it is not slavery I want to talk to you about, it is Joseph's wisdom, the way he knew to store grain, the way he devised a system to deliver it to all the people so that they did not have to suffer." He handed another piece of manna bread to Rana, and after she took it, he said, "You are one of the first to see the manna fall."

"Yes." Rana put a hand to her heart. "What a gift it was! Nearly as sweet as the wonderful manna itself."

"But unlike Joseph who built great storehouses for the grain, we cannot keep the manna day to day," Moses pointed out. "The Lord has told me if we try, the manna will rot and be inedible. It must be collected each day, and it occurs to me that it would be wise to have someone to take charge of the collection of it, as Joseph took charge of all the grain. We need to be sure those who are old or infirm and cannot leave their tents can still get their daily portion of manna. To check to see that those who might be greedy do not try and take too much."

"Yes." Rana nodded. "That makes a great deal of sense, though it sounds a difficult task. You will need someone—"

"As wise as our scholars," Moses says. "With the quick wits she developed on the streets."

The realization of all he proposed made Rana's stomach swoop. "You are not saying—"

Moses and Aaron exchanged looks. "We have discussed it. It is exactly what I am saying."

"But..." She stumbled over the words because she could not think straight, and when they finally popped out of her, she said, "But I deserve to be punished, not honored like this."

Moses laughed. "Oh, believe me, I think this will be punishment enough! Think of it, all the women gossiping while they gather manna each morning. All the mewling children. All the people who have to be assured their neighbors did not get one more grain of manna than they did. It will not be easy, but I cannot think of anyone here in our camp more fitted for the task."

Rana's heart swelled with gratitude, and her head whirled with possibilities. "I can choose those I wish to help me?" she asked.

"Not Leah the spinner." Moses's voice was warm even though he wagged a finger at her. "The thread she makes is too valuable and beautiful. I do not want her to stop spinning."

"I was thinking of Keziah," Rana told him. "She knows everyone in camp. And she knows everything about everyone. She will know who is ill and needs someone to grind their manna for them.

She will know who is too weak to go out and collect manna for themselves, and she knows enough people she can recruit to help do that."

"Perfect." Moses stood. "I will inform the leaders of the twelve tribes that you have agreed to my offer. It seems fitting, don't you think? Joseph the Hebrew once meted out grain to the Egyptians. And now an Egyptian will distribute manna to the Hebrews."

"I am grateful to the Lord God," Rana told him, and she spun toward the door. "And eager to share the news!"

She did not need to go far to do it.

Gideon was outside the tent, waiting for her.

Just as she trusted he would be.

FROM THE AUTHOR

Dear Reader,

I've never met a person who doesn't know the story of the Hebrew slaves and how they were led out of Egypt by Moses. We've all heard about the parting of the waters of the Red Sea, the wondrous pillar of fire and cloud that showed the Hebrews the way through the desert, the story of manna raining down from the sky—a miracle!

What that means, of course, is that when I decided to tackle the telling of the story in the pages of this book, I had to take a long, hard look at everything I knew about the Exodus and decide where my focus should be. I've been writing long enough to know better than to try and tell the entire story. That's just too overwhelming. Instead, I had to find a story that was small and personal and yet, encompassed the Exodus, a story that spoke to the heart of what happened out there in the wilderness so many thousands of years ago.

I found that when I realized that, like so many other stories in the Bible, this one is really about people.

These weren't just nameless slaves departing Egypt. They weren't just Hebrews trekking through the wasteland and on toward the Promised Land. These were people, real people, with lives and hopes and dreams. People with families and friends and problems. People like all of us.

At the center of it all is Rana, an Egyptian who joins the Exodus by chance. Rana is an outsider, and by having her as the central character who needs to learn the ways of the Hebrew people, I hope I've provided a way for all of us to get a look at what daily life out there in the wilderness might have been like. The challenges the Hebrews met, the disappointments that must have dogged their footsteps.

Those people had astounding faith and amazing perseverance, and looking at their lives through that lens gave me a chance to create a community of characters who, I hope, ring true in every way. Honoring their memory, their grit, and their unwavering belief in God made me more fully appreciate how their faithfulness runs in the veins of all who believe.

Anne Davidson

KEEPING THE FAITH

1. During their time in the wilderness, the Hebrews often talked about returning to Egypt. Why? What does their desire to go back into slavery tell all of us about our own tendencies to repeat patterns of unhealthy/harmful/unfaithful behavior?
2. Their time in the wilderness taught the Hebrews that their newfound freedom came with uncertainty and challenges. How were they able to keep their faith and stay obedient to God?
3. What can we learn from God's law pertaining to how much manna could be gathered and stored each day?
4. How does God's gift of manna relate to the teachings of Jesus?

BREAD OF TRUST: THE MIRACLE OF MANNA

By Reverend Jane Willan MS, MDiv

Imagine being part of a group of people who have left their old lives behind, driven by a common hope of a fresh start. At first, there's excitement and anticipation. But as days turn into weeks and the harshness of the journey sets in, hope begins to wane. The food supply is dwindling, and the once-optimistic people fall into despair.

This was the reality for the Israelites. Having escaped slavery in Egypt, they now faced a new oppressor—starvation. Grumbling, doubt, and anxiety spread among them. Had they made a terrible mistake?

In this dire situation, God provided a remarkable solution. One morning, the Israelites awoke to find the ground covered in small flakes. They looked at each other in confusion and asked, "What is this?" In Hebrew, the question "what is this" sounds like "man hu," which is where the word "manna" comes from.

Moses explained to the Israelites that this mysterious substance was food sent by God. Exodus 16:31 tells us that it was "white like coriander seed and tasted like wafers made with honey."

Numbers 11:7–8 adds that it "looked like resin," and that the people ground it up and either cooked it in a pot or made it into loaves, which "tasted like something made with olive oil." Doesn't sound too bad, does it?

But here's where it gets interesting. Instead of providing a lifetime supply of manna all at once, God sent it daily—in fact, it melted away in the heat of the sun—and set up specific guidelines for how to gather it. These rules were designed to test the Israelites' faith and obedience.

God instructed them to collect only enough manna for each day. This might seem straightforward, but it required a significant amount of trust. Imagine being told you can only gather enough food for today with no guarantee for tomorrow. Wouldn't you be tempted to hoard a little extra, just in case? Many Israelites did. Some even tried to keep manna overnight, despite the Lord's instructions. As a result, the manna turned foul, full of maggots and stinking. This wasn't just a lesson in trust but also a practical demonstration of constant reliance on God.

This daily provision of manna was a precursor to a teaching many of us know from the Lord's Prayer: "Give us this day our daily bread." Jesus was likely echoing this ancient lesson on trusting God for our needs, one day at a time.

On the sixth day of each week, the Israelites were instructed to gather a double portion of manna. This extra amount would not spoil overnight, allowing them to rest on the Sabbath without needing to collect food. This rule was another test of their faith, requiring them to trust God's provision and embrace the Sabbath.

Again, the response was mixed. While many followed the instructions and enjoyed the double portion on the sixth day, some went out on the Sabbath to gather more, only to find nothing. God's response was direct: "How long will you refuse to keep my commands and my instructions? Bear in mind that the Lord has given you the Sabbath; that is why on the sixth day he gives you bread for two days" (Exodus 16:28–29).

The only other manna that didn't spoil was the single serving Moses had his brother Aaron collect in a jar. This was kept with the tablets of the covenant law, so future generations would be able to see how the Lord had provided in the wilderness.

While the manna was the primary miraculous food provided to the Israelites in the wilderness, there was also another in the form of quail. According to Exodus 16:13, "That evening quail came and covered the camp, and in the morning, there was a layer of dew around the camp." This occurred just before the first appearance of manna, suggesting that God was addressing the Israelites' need for both meat and bread.

The quail incident wasn't a singular occurrence. Numbers 11 recounts another episode when God provided quail for the Israelites. During their forty-year wandering in the desert, the people had been complaining about the lack of meat in their diet, reminiscing about their food in Egypt. In response, God promised to give them meat, not just for a day but for a whole month. God caused a strong wind to bring quail from the sea, just as He said He would. The birds fell all around the camp, about three feet deep on the ground, covering an area as far as a day's walk in any direction. The Israelites greedily gathered the quail in abundance.

However, this event also came with a judgment, as many who had craved the meat were struck with a severe plague. This part of the story warns us about the dangers of being greedy and ungrateful, rather than trusting the Lord's perfect provision. It's a sharp contrast to the manna, which was all about learning to trust and rely on God's daily care.

God's provisions in the wilderness resonate throughout the Bible, pointing to deeper spiritual truths. In Deuteronomy 8:3, Moses reflects on the experience, saying, "He humbled you, causing you to hunger and then feeding you with manna, which neither you nor your ancestors had known, to teach you that man does not live on bread alone but on every word that comes from the mouth of the Lord."

Jesus references this teaching when tempted in the wilderness (Matthew 4:4), using it to highlight that true nourishment comes from God. Later, Jesus describes Himself as the true bread from heaven (John 6:32–35), linking the manna to His role as the sustainer of spiritual life.

God served up a profound lesson in faith and reliance for the Israelites when He gave them manna. More than just a solution to physical hunger, it was a daily exercise in trust and obedience. For people of faith today, the manna narrative reminds us that our deepest needs are met not through our own efforts but through a trusting relationship with God. He will always provide for us in His divine plan.

Fiction Author

ANNE DAVIDSON

Over the course of a thirty-plus-year writing career, Anne Davidson has published everything from newspaper articles to novels. *Sweet Gift from Heaven: Rana's Story* is the first story she's set in ancient times, and she was grateful to have the chance to examine the story of the Hebrew exodus from a new perspective. Anne lives in northeast Ohio with her husband and their two dogs. When she's not writing, she enjoys digging into family history and exploring old cemeteries, where she always finds beautiful art, interesting names, and inspiration for new books.

Nonfiction Author

REVEREND JANE WILLAN, MS, MDiv

Reverend Jane Willan writes contemporary women's fiction, mystery novels, church newsletters, and a weekly sermon.

Jane loves to set her novels amid church life. She believes that ecclesiology, liturgy, and church lady drama make for twisty plots and quirky characters. When not working at the church or creating new adventures for her characters, Jane relaxes at her favorite local bookstore, enjoying coffee and a variety of carbohydrates with frosting. Otherwise, you might catch her binge-watching a streaming series or hiking through the Connecticut woods with her husband and rescue dog, Ollie.

Jane earned a Bachelor of Arts degree from Hiram College, majoring in Religion and History, a Master of Science degree from Boston University, and a Master of Divinity from Vanderbilt University.

A NOTE FROM THE EDITORS

We hope you enjoyed another exciting volume in the Mysteries & Wonders of the Bible series, published by Guideposts. For over seventy-five years, Guideposts, a nonprofit organization, has been driven by a vision of a world filled with hope. We aspire to be the voice of a trusted friend, a friend who makes you feel more hopeful and connected.

By making a purchase from Guideposts, you join our community in touching millions of lives, inspiring them to believe that all things are possible through faith, hope, and prayer. Your continued support allows us to provide uplifting resources to those in need. Whether through our communities, websites, apps, or publications, we inspire our audiences, bring them together, and comfort, uplift, entertain, and guide them. Visit us at guideposts.org to learn more.

We would love to hear from you. Write us at Guideposts, P.O. Box 5815, Harlan, Iowa 51593 or call us at (800) 932-2145. Did you love *Sweet Gift from Heaven: Rana's Story*? Leave a review for this product on guideposts.org/shop. Your feedback helps others in our community find relevant products.

Find inspiration, find faith, find Guideposts.

Shop our best sellers and favorites at
guideposts.org/shop

Or scan the QR code to go directly to our Shop

If you enjoyed Mysteries & Wonders of the Bible, check out our other Guideposts biblical fiction series! Visit https://www.shopguideposts.org/fiction-books/biblical-fiction.html for more information.

EXTRAORDINARY WOMEN OF THE BIBLE

There are many women in Scripture who do extraordinary things. Women whose lives and actions were pivotal in shaping their world as well as the world we know today. In each volume of Guideposts' Extraordinary Women of the Bible series, you'll meet these well-known women and learn their deepest thoughts, fears, joys, and secrets. Read their stories and discover the unexplored truths in their journeys of faith as they follow the paths God laid out for them.

Highly Favored: Mary's Story
Sins as Scarlet: Rahab's Story
A Harvest of Grace: Ruth and Naomi's Story
At His Feet: Mary Magdalene's Story
Tender Mercies: Elizabeth's Story
Woman of Redemption: Bathsheba's Story
Jewel of Persia: Esther's Story
A Heart Restored: Michal's Story

Beauty's Surrender: Sarah's Story
The Woman Warrior: Deborah's Story
The God Who Sees: Hagar's Story
The First Daughter: Eve's Story
The Ones Jesus Loved: Mary and Martha's Story
The Beginning of Wisdom: Bilqis's Story
The Shadow's Song: Mahlah and No'ah's Story
Days of Awe: Euodia and Syntyche's Story
Beloved Bride: Rachel's Story
A Promise Fulfilled: Hannah's Story

ORDINARY WOMEN OF THE BIBLE

From generation to generation and every walk of life, God seeks out women to do His will. Scripture offers us but fleeting, tantalizing glimpses into the lives of a number of everyday women in Bible times—many of whom are not even named in its pages. In each volume of Guideposts' Ordinary Women of the Bible series, you'll meet one of these unsung, ordinary women face to face, and see how God used her to change the course of history.

A Mother's Sacrifice: Jochebed's Story
The Healer's Touch: Tikva's Story
The Ark Builder's Wife: Zarah's Story
An Unlikely Witness: Joanna's Story
The Last Drop of Oil: Adaliah's Story
A Perilous Journey: Phoebe's Story
Pursued by a King: Abigail's Story
An Eternal Love: Tabitha's Story
Rich Beyond Measure: Zlata's Story
The Life Giver: Shiphrah's Story
No Stone Cast: Eliyanah's Story
Her Source of Strength: Raya's Story
Missionary of Hope: Priscilla's Story

Befitting Royalty: Lydia's Story
The Prophet's Songbird: Atarah's Story
Daughter of Light: Charilene's Story
The Reluctant Rival: Leah's Story
The Elder Sister: Miriam's Story
Where He Leads Me: Zipporah's Story
The Dream Weaver's Bride: Asenath's Story
Alone at the Well: Photine's Story
Raised for a Purpose: Talia's Story
Mother of Kings: Zemirah's Story
The Dearly Beloved: Apphia's Story

**Interested in other series by Guideposts?
Check out one of our mystery series!
Visit https://www.shopguideposts.org/fiction-books/
mystery-fiction.html for more information.**

SECRETS FROM GRANDMA'S ATTIC

Life is recorded not only in decades or years, but in events and memories that form the fabric of our being. Follow Tracy Doyle, Amy Allen, and Robin Davisson, the granddaughters of the recently deceased centenarian, Pearl Allen, as they explore the treasures found in the attic of Grandma Pearl's Victorian home, nestled near the banks of the Mississippi in Canton, Missouri. Not only do Pearl's descendants uncover a long-buried mystery at every attic exploration, they also discover their grandmother's legacy of deep, abiding faith, which has shaped and guided their family through the years. These uncovered Secrets from Grandma's Attic reveal stories of faith, redemption, and second chances that capture your heart long after you turn the last page.

History Lost and Found
The Art of Deception
Testament to a Patriot
Buttoned Up

Pearl of Great Price
Hidden Riches
Movers and Shakers
The Eye of the Cat
Refined by Fire
The Prince and the Popper
Something Shady
Duel Threat
A Royal Tea
The Heart of a Hero
Fractured Beauty
A Shadowy Past
In Its Time
Nothing Gold Can Stay
The Cameo Clue
Veiled Intentions
Turn Back the Dial
A Marathon of Kindness
A Thief in the Night
Coming Home

SAVANNAH SECRETS

Welcome to Savannah, Georgia, a picture-perfect Southern city known for its manicured parks, moss-covered oaks, and antebellum architecture. Walk down one of the cobblestone streets, and you'll come upon Magnolia Investigations. It is here where two friends have joined forces to unravel some of Savannah's deepest secrets. Tag along as clues are exposed, red herrings discarded, and thrilling surprises revealed. Find inspiration in the special bond between Meredith Bellefontaine and Julia Foley. Cheer the friends on as they listen to their hearts and rely on their faith to solve each new case that comes their way.

The Hidden Gate
A Fallen Petal
Double Trouble
Whispering Bells
Where Time Stood Still
The Weight of Years
Willful Transgressions
Season's Meetings
Southern Fried Secrets
The Greatest of These

Patterns of Deception
The Waving Girl
Beneath a Dragon Moon
Garden Variety Crimes
Meant for Good
A Bone to Pick
Honeybees & Legacies
True Grits
Sapphire Secret
Jingle Bell Heist
Buried Secrets
A Puzzle of Pearls
Facing the Facts
Resurrecting Trouble
Forever and a Day

MYSTERIES OF MARTHA'S VINEYARD

Priscilla Latham Grant has inherited a lighthouse! So with not much more than a strong will and a sore heart, the recent widow says goodbye to her lifelong Kansas home and heads to the quaint and historic island of Martha's Vineyard, Massachusetts. There, she comes face-to-face with adventures, which include her trusty canine friend, Jake, three delightful cousins she didn't know she had, and Gerald O'Bannon, a handsome Coast Guard captain—plus head-scratching mysteries that crop up with surprising regularity.

A Light in the Darkness
Like a Fish Out of Water
Adrift
Maiden of the Mist
Making Waves
Don't Rock the Boat
A Port in the Storm
Thicker Than Water
Swept Away
Bridge Over Troubled Waters
Smoke on the Water
Shifting Sands

Shark Bait
Seascape in Shadows
Storm Tide
Water Flows Uphill
Catch of the Day
Beyond the Sea
Wider Than an Ocean
Sheeps Passing in the Night
Sail Away Home
Waves of Doubt
Lifeline
Flotsam & Jetsam
Just Over the Horizon

More Great Mysteries Are Waiting for Readers Like *You*!

Whistle Stop Café

"Memories of a lifetime...I loved reading this story. Could not put the book down...." —ROSE H.

Mystery and WWII historical fiction fans will love these intriguing novels where two close friends piece together clues to solve mysteries past and present. Set in the real town of Dennison, Ohio, at a historic train depot where many soldiers set off for war, these stories are filled with faithful, relatable characters you'll love spending time with.

Extraordinary Women of the Bible

"This entire series is a wonderful read.... Gives you a better understanding of the Bible." —SHARON A.

Now, in these riveting stories, you can get to know the most extraordinary women of the Bible, from Rahab and Esther to Bathsheba, Ruth, and more. Each book perfectly combines biblical facts with imaginative storylines to bring these women to vivid life and lets you witness their roles in God's great plan. These stories reveal how we can find the courage and faith needed today to face life's trials and put our trust in God just as they did.

Secrets of Grandma's Attic

"I'm hooked from beginning to end. I love how faith, hope, and prayer are included...[and] the scripture references... in the book at the appropriate time each character needs help. —JACQUELINE

Take a refreshing step back in time to the real-life town of Canton, Missouri, to the late Pearl Allen's home. Hours of page-turning intrigue unfold as her granddaughters uncover family secrets and treasures in their grandma's attic. You'll love seeing how faith has helped shape Pearl's family for generations.

Learn More & Shop These Exciting Mysteries, Biblical Stories & Other Uplifting Fiction at **guideposts.org/fiction**